D1535344

CREATING THE AGILE LIBRARY

Creating the Agile Library

A MANAGEMENT GUIDE
FOR LIBRARIANS

EDITED BY

Lorraine J. Haricombe
and T. J. Lusher

THE GREENWOOD LIBRARY MANAGEMENT COLLECTION
Gerard B. McCabe, *Series Adviser*

GREENWOOD PRESS
Westport, Connecticut • London

Library of Congress Cataloging-in-Publication Data

Creating the agile library : a management guide for librarians /
   edited by Lorraine J. Haricombe and T. J. Lusher.
      p.   cm.—(The Greenwood library management collection, ISSN
0894–2986)
    Includes bibliographical references and index.
    ISBN 0–313–30323–1 (alk. paper)
    1. Library administration—United States.   I. Haricombe, Lorraine
J.   II. Lusher, T. J., 1963– .   III. Series.
   Z678.C757   1998
   025.1—dc21   97–40854

British Library Cataloguing in Publication Data is available.

Library of Congress Catalog Card Number: 97–40854
ISBN: 0–313–30323–1
ISSN: 0894–2986

First published in 1998

Greenwood Press, 88 Post Road West, Westport, CT 06881
An imprint of Greenwood Publishing Group, Inc.

Printed in the United States of America

∞™

The paper used in this book complies with the
Permanent Paper Standard issued by the National
Information Standards Organization (Z39.48–1984).

10 9 8 7 6 5 4 3 2

Contents

Preface

W. Bede Mitchell

In such a world, happiness is inconceivable. How can it dwell where, as Plato says, "continual Becoming and never Being" is the sole form of existence?

> Arthur Schopenhauer, "Vanity of Existence" (1892?, 395–396)

There is a certain relief in change, even though it be from bad to worse; as I have found in travelling in a stage-coach, that it is often a comfort to shift one's position and be bruised in a new place.

> Washington Irving, *Tales of a Traveller* (1987, 4–5)

In 1979, Miriam Drake wrote, "Until recently, librarians have had the luxury of living in a relatively certain and risk-free environment" (507). The academic library was supposedly the heart of the institution, an intellectual resource whose value to higher education was unquestioned and whose environment was relatively stable and well understood. In hindsight, it appears the academic library was refining and perfecting a paradigm, a paradigm that began to be overturned shortly before the time Drake wrote the words above. This book is an attempt to help academic libraries respond to changes in that paradigm. By becoming agile libraries, we may be better prepared to manage and respond to necessary change.

Thomas Kuhn's theory of scientific paradigms has become very familiar since he published it in the 1962 monograph *The Structure of Scientific Revolutions*. Kuhn developed the theory to explain that science, rather than being a steady, cumulative acquisition of knowledge, was in fact a series of successive and violent revolutions. His theory of science has since been adapted to a number of other disciplines and situations, and certainly many writers in the academic library literature have found it to be a powerful model of what is happening in our field. In this very volume, Kuhn's theory is aptly cited and applied in Chapter 1 by Fred Heath and the Introduction by editors Lorraine J. Haricombe and T. J. Lusher.

According to Kuhn, scientists are trained within a prevailing paradigm, a fundamental, overarching explanation of a scientific problem. The paradigm provides the basis for further work within the discipline, with most scientists focusing on extending the scope of the paradigm. For example, the Big Bang theory provides the paradigm for contemporary cosmologists and physicists. The predominant work in those fields involves finding solutions to unresolved questions implicit in or deduced from the Big Bang theory.

In light of Miriam Drake's assessment and Kuhn's theory, we might say that libraries until the 1960s or 1970s were primarily refining and extending a paradigm of library science and service that grew out of the work of Melvil Dewey and other library pioneers of the late nineteenth and early twentieth centuries. Their paradigm was a response to the social, economic, and educational environment of their time. In the view of many, that environment has been replaced; the academic world in which we now work has undergone a paradigm shift. A new paradigm of higher education is forcing in turn a change in, or perhaps a shift from, the traditional library science paradigm. These changes are occurring, in Kuhn's terms, because difficulties within the old paradigm have stimulated revolutionary thinkers to break away from the paradigm and develop new means to deal with the difficulties that could not be solved within the old paradigm. Lorraine J. Haricombe and T. J. Lusher state in this volume's Introduction, ''The impact of technology has generated a paradigm shift in higher education. Changes such as curricular structures, remote access to education, and instructional delivery have spurred serious debates about the role of teaching in the future.'' Many believe that academic libraries cannot meet these and similar challenges by simply refining and extending the old library science paradigm. However, the shift to a new paradigm is fraught with problems and dangers.

In a complex system like a library, with its web of varied and sometimes conflicting patron needs, diverse staff and faculty personalities, and myriad workflows and procedures, the outcomes of decisions can be affected in countless ways by unanticipated factors. According to chaos theory, both complex and simple systems are subject to unpredictable circumstances which in turn affect our actions in unpredictable ways. Consider the following from the *Encyclopedia Britannica*'s entry on chaos:

For example, the meteorologist Edward Lorenz discovered that a simple model of heat convection possesses intrinsic unpredictability, a circumstance he called the ''butterfly effect,'' suggesting that the mere flapping of a butterfly's wing can change the weather. A more homely example is the pinball machine: the ball's movements are precisely governed by laws of gravitational rolling and elastic collisions—both fully understood— yet the final outcome is unpredictable.

Failure to appreciate this fact can lead to frustration and disillusionment on the part of library managers whose best-laid plans for effecting and managing change do not turn out as expected.

Kuhn believed that a new paradigm is not built on the preceding paradigm because the two are "incommensurable," but rather the new supplants the old. In this light, it is understandable when people suggest, as have several on my own campus, that it is pointless and wasteful to erect new library buildings since in the paperless society of the future (the new paradigm as they see it), all information will be on-line and we will only need a room full of computer workstations to serve as a library. Such dramatic and revolutionary change is usually traumatic and disruptive, requiring a willingness to take risks and endure the consequences of missteps. Institutions making the move to a new paradigm may not have experience with this kind of "whitewater rafting." Drake pointed out that as libraries enter a period of uncertainty,

a natural tendency is to try to conserve what is at hand rather than invest for future gain. Project selection and the process of the individual projects also contain elements of uncertainty. With many projects from which to choose and fuzzy measures of payoff and benefit/cost, management has to live with the idea that the projects chosen may not turn out to have been the best selections. (1979, 507)

Thus, if Kuhn's theory is applicable to this period in academic library history, it will not do to simply hunker down, conserving and adapting our past to the requirements of the present. We must seek radically new and sometimes risky solutions and be prepared to live with our mistakes, whether they are of judg- ment or are due to the flapping of butterfly wings. But the implication that we must somehow start from scratch, because the old and new paradigms are in- commensurable, is very troubling to librarians like Walt Crawford and Michael Gorman.

In their 1995 book *Future Libraries: Dreams, Madness, & Reality*, Crawford and Gorman state that ''The library of tomorrow must be one that retains not only the best of the past but also a sense of the history of libraries and of human communication. Without that, the library will be purely reactive, a thing of the moment, sometimes useful and sometimes not but never central to human so- ciety'' (12). Perhaps our fear of becoming obsolete is leading us to embrace new technologies and philosophies that are undermining a system of library values and service which has been extremely successful and needs fine-tuning, not overhauling.

In my view, Crawford and Gorman sound a healthy cautionary note and provide an important historical context for considering how the traditional values and mission of academic libraries should be the basis for meeting the paradigm shift head on. And as the chapters in this volume will attempt to demonstrate, the concept of the agile institution may offer us the opportunity to learn to adjust to change by building on and adapting existing strengths and core values. In the words of agile organization authorities Goldman, Nagel, and Preiss, agile industries "not only understand their *current* markets, product lines, competencies, and customers very well, they also understand the potential for *future* customers and markets. This understanding leads to strategic plans to acquire new competencies, develop new product lines, and open up new markets" (1995, 42). Haricombe, Lusher, and their colleagues are offering us a guide to adapting these principles of organizational agility to our libraries.

In short, change is a reality of life and whether it is paradigmatic or incremental, it must be met. Drake wrote that "An innovative environment calls for new skills in risk assessment, ability to understand uncertainty, and ability to manage increased entrepreneurial activity" (1979, 507). The concept of the agile library is one of an adaptable, responsive, and innovative institution. According to Goldman, Nagel, and Preiss, "Agility is dynamic, context-specific, aggressively change-embracing, and growth-oriented. It is *not* about improving efficiency, cutting costs, or battening down the business hatches to ride out fearsome competitive 'storms.' . . . There is no point at which a company or an individual has completed the journey to agility" (1995, 42). In other words, the agile organization is "continually becoming," in Plato's terms. It is positioned to "aggressively embrace change. For agile competitors—people as well as companies—change and uncertainty are self-renewing sources of opportunities out of which to fashion continuing change" (Goldman, Nagel, and Preiss 1995, 43).

It is clear we live in "interesting times." How we in academic libraries can thrive in such times is not so clear. Let us turn now with an open mind to the text and see in greater detail what we can learn from agile organizations.

REFERENCES

Crawford, Walt, and Michael Gorman. 1995. *Future Libraries: Dreams, Madness, & Reality*. Chicago: American Library Association.

Drake, Miriam. 1979. "Managing Innovation in Academic Libraries." *College and Research Libraries* 40, 6 (November): 503–510.

Encyclopedia Britannica. A web publication. See http://www.eb.com.

Goldman, Steven L., Roger N. Nagel, and Kenneth Preiss. 1995. *Agile Competitors and Virtual Organizations: Strategies for Enriching the Customer*. New York: Van Nostrand Reinhold.

Irving, Washington. 1987. [reprint] *Tales of a Traveller*. Boston: Twayne.

Kuhn, Thomas. 1970. *The Structure of Scientific Revolutions*. Chicago: University of Chicago Press.

Schopenhauer, Arthur. 1892? "Vanity of Existence." In *Essays of Arthur Schopenhauer*. New York: A. L. Burt.

Acknowledgments

The idea for this publication arose from our presentation at the ACRL 7th National Conference in Pittsburgh, Pennsylvania. Our enthusiasm to bring the publication to fruition was fueled by the many questions and comments we received after our ACRL presentation. We thank those individuals who directly and indirectly helped to shape the idea for the work. In particular, we thank all the contributors for their invaluable insights and perspectives. It is our hope that the publication will generate more discussion and provide ideas for managing the future library.

Finally, we would be remiss if we did not thank Vicky Smith for her assistance in typing and formatting the manuscript.

Introduction

It is often said that change is the only constant. This change is all around us, and the rate at which it occurs is faster than ever before. As we approach the end of the twentieth century, few can dispute that a large measure of the transformations are the result of advances in technology. With its ever-present drive for faster and better ways to process and disseminate information, technology is fueling changes in society at large and in academia especially.

The impact of technology has generated a paradigm shift in higher education. Changes such as curricular structures, remote access to education, and instructional delivery have spurred serious debates about the role of teaching in the future. At the same time, other changes have occurred that will affect the future planning of higher education. Increasingly, schools are reaching out to a growing market of adult students by providing continuing education at remote sites. Consequently, distance education centers are dotting the higher education landscape.

Corollary to the debates about the future role of traditional teaching methods and teaching venues is the question of what role the library will and should occupy. The shifting paradigm in higher education, combined with new and emerging technologies, will continue to impact the academic library. Transforming libraries to respond to these changes is a major but necessary undertaking if they are to remain central to the mission of education. Responding to the changes will require academic libraries to become more user-centered. Being user-centered enables the library to know its users and to assess their needs, but that alone is not enough. ''Today's effective library must embrace creativity, innovation and entrepreneurship. And it must provide an environment that encourages and supports risk taking!'' (Riggs 1996, 403). An agile organization permits the flexibility to take risks to make responsive changes that will address its users' needs.

In Chapter 1, Fred Heath introduces the concept of agility in the for-profit sector. He draws a parallel between the mass production era and self-sufficient libraries to show the applicability of the agility model for libraries. Agility allowed visionary corporate leaders to assess threats to their companies' survival and to take the opportunity to make changes to ensure their success. In the same way, libraries need to heed the shifting paradigm in higher education and the continuing advances in technology to make relevant changes.

Preparing the organization for change is a prerequisite inasmuch as the need for implementing change is a challenge. In Chapter 2, Rebecca R. Martin discusses the role of strong leadership to create and nurture an agile environment that will permit planning for change while dealing with daily operations.

New and emerging technologies allow libraries to construct library services and products to address the needs of current and future users. In Chapter 3, T. J. Lusher provides an overview of how to plan a technologically agile library. Using a technology plan permits the library to identify its technological strengths and weaknesses and implement changes to address the needs of its users.

Using case studies, Clifton Dale Foster and Steven J. Bell focus in Chapter 4 on the feasibility of wireless communication technologies to provide flexibility in connecting people with information "anytime, anywhere." Their chapter provides useful information about the basic types of wireless transfer technologies for library applications and their future possibilities.

In an environment of continuous change, libraries are moving closer to a virtual environment of access and service. In Chapter 5, Thomas A. Peters discusses the challenges of identifying and measuring outcomes in an emerging virtual environment. He focuses on outcome measures for public services and provides an overview of management tools that may be useful to measure outcomes in virtual libraries. He concludes that, to remain meaningful, user-centered outcome measures will become a crucial way to assess the value of virtual libraries.

All too often, the forgotten element in future planning of the academic library is the user. In Chapter 6, Lorraine J. Haricombe identifies several factors that affect the type of user population the library will serve in the future. Choosing the most appropriate response to future users' needs will require that libraries examine their clientele profile and be sensitive to changing trends in their user population.

Libraries no longer have the monopoly in the information infrastructure. To retain its centrality in higher education requires that libraries adopt a more creative and flexible approach to meet the information needs of their constituents. In Chapter 7, Darlene E. Weingand addresses the importance of using tools to identify the users' needs and to develop healthy partnerships with the various constituent groups. The best intentions of the library will be lost unless its constituents know and perceive them as benefits to themselves.

The library is an open system that depends on external resources and technology to provide products and services to its users. An adjustment in any one of the variables has a snowball effect on the entire system. Ongoing changes in higher education, technology, user population, and resources will impact the library's role, mission, and goals. Libraries cannot remain passive. This book is intended to be a ''thinking tool'' for library managers as they prepare to create, harness, and manage continuous change in their libraries.

REFERENCE

Riggs, Donald E. 1996. ''Creating and Managing Change: Some Controversy, Some Level-Headedness.'' *College and Research Libraries* 57, 5: 402–404.

CREATING THE AGILE LIBRARY

1

The Agile Organization: A "Better Mousetrap" for Libraries?

Fred Heath

BACKGROUND

The literature of management theory and practice is a literature of fashion. While the life span of concepts may vary, the manner in which they ascend to popularity, gain credibility, and then inexorably make their way across the landscape follows similar patterns. Whether it is management by objectives, zero defects, Theory Y, strategic planning, Total Quality Management (TQM), Continuous Improvement, or the Learning Organization, they seem to follow a very similar pattern. Usually they emerge in the for-profit sector and in the manner of toppling dominos move steadily through the government agencies, and then rattle around in education. Libraries may represent the last domino in line; announcement of the release of a book on *Strategic Planning and Libraries* or whatever may signal that some other *concept* has already captured the attention of the commercial sector. The dominos are set back up and the process begins anew.

Thomas Burgess acknowledges that management literature is "bedeviled" by hype and is often greeted by academics and practitioners alike with a healthy dose of skepticism (Burgess 1994, 23). Yet, by and large, each of these concepts or models offers better ways of doing things. Certainly, it is reasonable that they arise in economic sectors where the stakes can be measured in billions of dollars and human resources can be counted in the tens or hundreds of thousands of employees. And it is helpful that libraries have practitioners who assay the applications of new concepts to the not-for-profit way of doing things.

As yet, the concept of agility is not a broadly embraced or widely understood concept. Nevertheless, the theories wrapped up in the *agile enterprise* package are touted by their advocates as something ground-breaking. As one advocate proclaims: "Change is old news, but the idea of carefully engineering an enterprise to thrive in change is new. In fact, it's a radical idea" (*Metrics for the Agile Virtual Enterprise*).

Is this the breakthrough librarians have been seeking, or are library administrators—as are managers in every field—better served to regard *agility* as one more example of what Jim Govan (1977) called "better mousetraps"—potentially useful ideas that we should examine carefully and then employ as best fits the local situation? This chapter attempts to examine the concept of *the agile organization*, to evaluate the uniqueness of its contributions to the management literature, and to assess its applicability to the not-for-profit sector as well as to libraries specifically.

COMPETITION AND SURVIVAL: THE NEED FOR ADAPTABILITY

Agility is a recently enunciated management idea that undertakes to deal aggressively with change. The concept of the agile enterprise is one where in an environment of intense competition and unanticipated rapid change, an organization assesses threat, finds opportunities, and *prospers*. A flavor of the concept can be found in the following passage from the book *Agile Competitors and Virtual Organizations* (Goldman et al. 1995, xv–xvii):

Broader product ranges, shorter model lifetimes, and the ability to process orders in arbitrary lot sizes are becoming the norm. . . . The information processing capability to treat masses of customers as individuals is permitting more and more companies to offer individualized products while maintaining high volumes of production. The convergence of computer networking and telecommunications technologies is making it possible for groups of companies to coordinate geographically and institutionally distributed capabilities into a single *virtual company* and to achieve powerful competitive advantages in the process.

Agile competition is not someone's "great idea" of how businesses *ought* to be run; it is how more and more businesses, of all sizes and across all industries, *are being run* today in order to stay in business.

Simply put, survival requires adaptability in the face of unanticipated change. *Adaptability* is the key to survival. The agile enterprise is being touted as one of those better mousetraps, one of those management tools that will allow corporations to survive and prosper in fiercely competitive times. It is getting plenty of attention in the for-profit sector. General Motors is among the corporate giants who have enrolled their managers in the agile manufacturing program at Lehigh University's Iacocca Institute. One of their plant managers, who spent a year studying in the executive program there, was quick to find the relevance of the program to his Pittsburgh-area plant: "Driving alongside the riverbeds shows you why you should work hard. When you take that route, you see all of the once-thriving steel mills that have closed down. That gives me incentive to be more competitive and grow jobs at this plant. Our employees have seen so many plant closures, they don't want another one" (Moskal 1995, 12).

THE AGILE ENTERPRISE: AN OVERVIEW

Unlike prior times, when aggressive growth strategies were the hallmark of corporate strategies, the last ten years in the for-profit sector have been characterized by retrenchment and downsizing. Moreover, that trend has gone far beyond the corporations. Governments, higher education, hospitals, and the public sector generally have all been adversely affected by rising costs and declining revenues.

Dozens of studies have analyzed the decline of American industry. In 1991, Roger Nagel, operations director of the Lee Iacocca Institute at Lehigh University, spent the summer going over those studies with several executives from major U.S. corporations. They found the clues to industrial decline in the inherent weaknesses in the mass production model. The key to American wealth had been the assembly line, pouring out huge numbers of low-cost goods. The model, dating from Henry Ford and his revolutionary automobile plants, was extremely capital and machine intensive. Expensive equipment required that huge inventories be turned out to lower unit costs. The factories were necessarily unresponsive to consumer interests, unattuned to changing tastes or needs. Corporate practice was to keep the expensive production lines running, even if it meant piling up inventory.

In the immediate postwar years, the Japanese examined this model closely to find a means to compete against the well-capitalized West. They found it in the concept of *lean manufacturing*, rooted in Toyota's just-in-time production system (Burgess 1994, 24). Without the capital assets of the United States, the Japanese concentrated on processes which would allow inventory reductions. So advanced has the concept become that industry planners in Japan are sharpening the concept of the three-day automobile. The concept revolves around high-quality interchangeable parts that allow consumers to design their own automobile in the showroom out of available components, with the resulting effort delivered to the customer in only three days (Port 1992, 177; Sheridan 1993, 30–46). The tremendous reduction in inventories permitted profitability to soar. By the 1970s the Japanese were outperforming their U.S. competitors, presaging the American industrial decline of the 1980s.

Enter the concept of the agile enterprise. Agility crystallized as a strategic concept in 1991, when industrial executives became concerned that the pace of change in the business world was exceeding the capacity of manufacturing organizations to adapt. Sector-dominant corporations were suddenly failing as markets changed and customers found satisfaction in other outlets. Some of the corporations never awoke to the threats facing them and went straight down the drain. Others saw the threat and considered or attempted a remedy, but simply could not react with sufficient speed to survive.

The first articulation of *agile competition*, as it was then known, was Nagel's report out of the Lee Iacocca Institute at Lehigh University in the fall of 1991. The impetus had been a congressional request to determine how the United States could return to global competitiveness. Further, the initiative was at least in part a response to a Japanese study, *Manufacturing 21*, which sought to achieve the same thing for that nation's industrial sector (Sheridan 1993). The Lehigh report, *21st Century Manufacturing Enterprise Strategy: An Industry-Led View*, determined that an incremental improvement of the existing system was not enough to ensure success (Goldman et al. 1991). However, a new system of *agile production* was emerging, combining information, communication, and production technologies which would redefine the competitive marketplace (Goldman 1994, 43–47). The concept found support in higher education, at high levels in government agencies, and, most importantly, in industry. More than 25,000 copies of the report have been distributed. Consultants have emerged, and conferences, workshops, and seminars have been offered (Goldman et al. 1995, xxi). Among the leading spokespersons of the movement are Steven L. Goldman, Roger N. Nagel, and Kenneth Preiss. Their *Agile Competitors and Virtual Organizations* serves as an effective overview of the doctrine. For the authors (1995, xv-xvii), the dimensions of the agile enterprise can be explained as (1) customer enrichment through individualized "solutions" rather than "products" for the mass market; (2) cooperation which can enhance competitiveness; (3) the commitment to the mastery of change and uncertainty; and (4) recognition of the importance of people and information technologies and the determination to optimize the use of both.

By the winter of 1992, industry had established the Agile Manufacturing Enterprise Forum (AMEF). Created within the Lee Iacocca Institute at Lehigh University, its purpose was to continue to refine the concept of *agility* and further disseminate that concept widely throughout U.S. industry. By 1994, AMEF was operating under the name *Agility Forum*, and its publications and activities are fully accessible over the World Wide Web (Goldman et al. 1995, xxi).

The *Agility Forum* touts itself as "the leading provider of Agility knowledge, products, and consulting services to strengthen the U.S. economy" (*Agility Forum*). In a way, it is an American response to the Japanese-born initiatives of the 1970s and 1980s. Donald Runkle, vice president of the General Motors Advanced Engineering Staff, was glad that the job was finally accomplished:

I am more than a little disappointed that some great American university didn't research the fundamentals of manufacturing and actually invent lean production—before the Japanese did. . . . [W]hat's disturbing is that none of the nation's great research institutions managed to uncover the work being done on lean manufacturing and to teach its techniques in the mid-70s—when many of us who are now leading America's industry were in business school—trying to get an education. (Vasilash 1993, 58)

Hardly an original doctrine, Agility incorporates the best of the tools of the trade, including lean manufacturing, just-in-time, TQM, and the like (Moskal 1995, 14). Too, in a time of downsizing and cost-cutting, it is intended to provide an ebullient and upbeat message. As Edward A. Miller, president of the National Center for Manufacturing Sciences (Ann Arbor), said in 1992, the forum offered an opportunity to rethink the manufacturing infrastructure and assess the possibility of vaulting ahead of the Japanese once again (Port 1992, 177).

MASTERY OF CHANGE

According to its advocates, the agile enterprise is nothing less than the coming of a new order. "Being Agile," says Rick Dove, "means being proficient at change—and allows an organization to do anything it wants whenever it wants to" (Dove 1994, 14).

A key to the success of the agile enterprise, say the prophets, is time-sensitive responsiveness to customer needs. The Japanese concept of the three-day automobile is one example. The three-day suit is another. One author paints a scenario where customers enter an automated kiosk within which electronic equipment assesses relevant body parameters. From a screen, they select fabric and color choices. At a factory far remote, lasers cut the chosen fabric to precise computer-generated patterns. Far more quickly than a tailor could respond, the suit is available at Nordstrom's or other fine outlets (Port 1994, 158). Not possible? At a number of Original Levi's stores in the United States, women can be measured for a pair of jeans; from there the computerized measurements are sent to a Tennessee factory. Within three weeks, the jeans are back in the store, or, for a small fee, express mailed to the customer (Cooke 1995, 27).

Here, say some advocates, reside American prospects for success. The robustness of the U.S. information infrastructure facilitates communication from the production floor to the showroom. As one writer for *Business Week* put it:

advanced computer networks will serve as an infrastructure to connect essentially every factory, job shop, and industrial design studio—putting world-class experience just a computer call away. Companies will concentrate their resources on a few strategic processes and turn to on-line partners for everything else. (Port 1992, 180)

Dove and Goldman, leaders in the agility movement, agree. They believe that the Japanese ascendancy was based upon a mastery of the manufacturing process itself. But the need for speed as well as quality shifts the focus away from manufacturing to the knowledge of customer demands and the software which permits rapid response. According to the gurus, mastery of the information technologies could restore the American edge (Port 1994, 159).

SURVIVING RAPID CHANGE

It is that part of the definition of agility—surviving and prospering in a time of rapid change—that should interest us as librarians. To understand, it is necessary to move the concept of agility into the framework of libraries and scholarly communication. Whether bewildered by the pace of change or frustrated because the transition to a brighter electronic future seems to be taking so long, most librarians would agree that libraries are in the midst of a big change in the way business is conducted. If the manufacturing scenario depicts a paradigm shift from Fordist concepts of mass production to Japanese just-in-time and lean production practices, it should be possible to frame the information revolution to which we are witnesses within the context of two cultures: an old world of print media and particularly journal subscriptions and a new world, less clearly seen, in which electronic access to information in one guise or another will most certainly play a major part.

In his book *The Structure of Scientific Revolutions*, Thomas Kuhn (1970) explicates the concept of paradigm shifts, in which an ensconced paradigm struggles to hold sway and experiences frequent assaults before finally being supplanted by a new paradigm. Higher education is in the midst of a revolutionary period—the second such intellectual event of modern time—where an old paradigm is being assaulted and appears certain to yield to a new mode of scholarly communication. The first intellectual revolution was occasioned by moveable metal type, the invention of the modern printing press, attributed to Gutenberg sometime in the mid-1400s. With the advent of the modern press, information could be distributed far more widely, speedily, and economically. Ease of access to the printed word placed a new premium upon literacy. An old world—in which knowledge was a scarce commodity and the abilities to read and write were bestowed only upon an elite—over the next 100 years came crumbling down. The book replaced the manuscript. Literacy spread from the monastery to the marketplace, and contemporary civilization emerged. And just as the modern information age is marked by the rapid obsolescence of things around us, so it was in the aftermath of the printing revolution.

One of the earliest casualties of the first revolution was the old manuscript library. David Vaisey, Bodley's Librarian at Oxford University, visited Texas A&M recently. During his stay, he reminded his audience of one victim of that first transition. As it neared completion in the mid-fifteenth century, Oxford's Duke Humfrey's Library was to have set the standard for European universities at that time. But even as that splendid manuscript library was being built, it was on its way to becoming an anachronism. Gutenberg's printing press was making itself felt at the very same time. The advent of moveable type meant that the many colleges of Oxford could have their own copies of important works—in book form—splendidly and inexpensively mass produced, housed within their own colleges for use by faculty and students. A central repository of rare manuscripts was unnecessary, and Oxford's colleges quickly lost interest in funding its maintenance (Vaisey 1994). Unable to adapt to changing conditions and no longer satisfying its initial purpose, the library failed. Sixty-five years after it opened its doors, Duke Humfrey's library was abandoned and the manuscripts sold. Oxford would be without a central library until the great Bodleian Library opened its doors a half-century later (Rogers 1991, 51).

And from the rise of those early college libraries until not so long ago, academic libraries retained many similarities. Until the dawn of the second information revolution in the 1960s, a scholar engaged in time travel would have felt pretty much at home no matter where in the intervening centuries she may have stopped. The 1960s are selected as a demarcation date because the wave upon which libraries are now borne had its origin then, in the invention of the *integrated circuit*, a tiny device that controls electrical signals and makes possible the modern computer. The concept of the integrated circuit—perhaps better known as the *microchip*—has been around for some time; it was perfected in the 1960s by Jack Kilby and Robert Noyce. Their achievements may be perhaps the most significant breakthrough of the twentieth century. And while they are not well known now, in time, their names may be joined with Gutenberg's as the great facilitators of the modern information age (Everhart 1993).

It is the integrated circuit industry that is driving the revolution in information technologies, giving us the computers that allow us to process and distribute information in all forms at speeds heretofore unimaginable. Thomas Everhart (1993) recalls that as a young man, he worked in 1954 at Hughes Aircraft and struggled to operate a giant, unfriendly, first-generation computer which the corporation rented for thousands of dollars monthly. Today, he reminds us, we can buy personal computers—which are truly a thousand times more powerful than that first model—for under $1,000. That, he says, represents an improvement in cost effectiveness of more than 10 million times.

THE IMPACT OF THE REVOLUTION UPON LIBRARIES

Just as industrialists recognize that the competitive model of the mass-production era is behind them, so too must libraries recognize that the self-sufficient research library, containing on its shelves the universe of print materials required to support the university mission, is an anachronism. As we have seen in the example of Duke Humfrey's Library, rapid shifts in the environment displaced manuscript libraries from their niche. Do today's developments in the information technologies offer a similar threat?

Louis Rossetto, editor of *Wired* magazine and multimedia visionary, certainly seems to feel that a new world is already imminent. The electronic, on-line world, he says, is more in keeping with humankind's oral tradition. It is the print world that was the aberration; written information deposited in libraries and read and re-read over the centuries is not germane to the breadth of the human experience. To his mind, the advent of the computer banishes the classroom and the library in preference to a better kind of future, where all information is linked worldwide, and there is an explosion in accessibility of knowledge to rival that in Gutenberg's day. It will of course be a far less orderly world, less concerned with the principles of organization which characterize the library today. Retrievability will be messier in cyberspace, and what one is looking for will not always be there at the first query. And there will be no gatekeepers, no navigators once the downramp onto the information highway is freely accessible. It is, says Rossetto, ''a direct connection of minds. Humans have always been isolated, and now we are starting to see electronic connections generating an intellectual organism of their own, literally a quantum leap beyond our experience with consciousness'' (Max 1994, 62). Anyone who can write can publish; anyone who can read can have access to written information and engage all who are interested in debate. Not just scholarly communications, but all communications will undergo a fundamental environmental change. In the parlance of agility, these developments represent a major threat to libraries, for they could be rendered irrelevant.

To these environmental pressures can be added economic factors. Everyone in this business of information transfer is aware of the economic problems confronting libraries over the past decade. The financial challenges have all but overwhelmed many universities. And it is not just a library problem, it is a financial issue which strikes at the very heart of higher education. In a recent address before an OCLC gathering in Dublin, Ohio, Brian Hawkins (1994), Vice President for Academic Planning at Brown University, offered his own perspective on the magnitude of the dilemma.

As his university attempted in the mid-1980s to position itself strategically for the rest of the century, its strategic planning effort focused upon the major ''budget busters'' which were draining available resources. By ''budget busters,'' Hawkins meant those activities which were increasing on the order of 200 percent for the decade. There were four items that were identified in the planning process:

• Financial aid
• Health care
• Development/Institutional advancement
• Libraries

And, Hawkins reported, Brown fashioned solutions for all of its problems except libraries.

The only solution Brown could find was to *throw money* at the problems of runaway library costs. Mr. Hawkins reported that Brown was among the lucky ones and was able over a decade to add incrementally to the library materials expenditures at a rate of about 8½ percent per annum.

The bad news, he said, was that Brown found that those hefty investment levels could not be sustainable indefinitely. Moreover, the real fact of the matter, Hawkins continued, was that even at that rather healthy rate of investment, the cost of library materials was rising even faster, and Brown University found its library's buying power falling further and further behind.

What Hawkins discovered was the grim reality of the steady decline in buying power that occurs when Brown invests in materials at one rate and library materials continue to increase in price at another. We know from recent studies that historically, the journal literature has grown at approximately 12 percent per annum. Not so far down the road, by 2010, Hawkins projected that his university library would be purchasing a mere 30 percent of what it could buy in 1980!

His projections worsened. He realized that the amount of information available for sale is skyrocketing. As he saw it, given the current rate of growth if the material the Brown library purchased in 1980 represented *everything* its academic community needed, then by the year 2010 they would be acquiring less than 1 percent of the information universe.

Is this depiction accurate? It probably is. Hawkins used a pretty conservative estimate of the rate at which information is growing. Recently, there have been suggestions that in the midst of the electronic revolution, with the ability of the machine to package and repackage information, the amount of information available to us is doubling on the order of every 18 months! Most librarians can agree with the estimate that ''more words are put out in a week by the 20 million people who use the Internet than are published by all major American publishing companies in a year'' (Max 1994, 67).

Yet, the problems confronting academic libraries may be more pernicious than an administrative officer like Mr. Hawkins perceives. Many libraries are going to be sorely tried by this transition from a print world to the electronic universe that is out there on the horizon. And at least during the transition period, the more nimble will enjoy the greatest success.

HOW LIBRARIES CAN RESPOND TO CHANGE AND THREAT

Agility precepts can serve to guide libraries through this period of rapid change that Rossetto and Hawkins have identified. In the parlance of the manufacturing sector, agility is something quite apart from just becoming better, faster, and cheaper, from becoming profitable today. In fact, a focus on profitability today may make the enterprise less agile. Back in 1993, Texas A&M Libraries reacted to the economic realities confronting it—so bleakly described by Hawkins—by the not-for-profit's equivalent of focusing on today's bottom line. Reacting to local funding situations and the continuing rise in the cost of journals, the Sterling C. Evans Libraries cut $435,000 of journal titles. Did that make the libraries more agile? Well, it balanced the bottom line, but it did nothing to address the library's campus niche as information provider to the colleges. "You generally need to be lean to be agile," says Rick Dove, a leading agility consultant, "but you don't want everything that lean brings to the table. If a plant gets as lean as it is possible to be, then it becomes extremely fragile to the impact of change. The ultimately lean organization is optimized for doing what it is doing—and nothing else. It is static" (Sheridan 1993, 30).

Deep journal cuts only staved off the next round of inflation-driven reductions in the budget cycle; it did nothing to prepare the library to invest in the solutions to client needs promised by the information technologies. The alternative to "off-the-shelf satisfaction" of information needs was replaced in too many instances with reliance upon mail-based interlibrary loan. The resultant decline in responsiveness hastened faculty reliance upon alternatives being opened up by Louis Rossetto's global information village. Far from positioning the libraries strategically, the enormous cuts threatened to set Evans Libraries upon the path of irrelevancy in the eyes of its constituents.

To succeed, say the advocates of agility, threats must be viewed as opportunity. Libraries must seek the avenues which permit them to prosper. The advocates remind would-be practitioners that at one level agility is simply the exercise of sound management practices. In particular, effective monitoring of customer expectations and needs is always helpful. Much can be done merely by heightening awareness and sensitivity, although a robust investment in assessment of customer needs is always a good place to start.

An important first step in the agility model is to *evaluate the organization.* Evaluate the vectors pushing on the library or other organization and determine in what direction they are likely to push. Ascertain the internal weaknesses and the external threats. What opportunities can be discerned?

A second step is to *assess the ability of the enterprise to respond.* Develop assessments of the time and costs to change given the specific context of the organization. What are the strengths of the organization that can be called upon?

The third step in the agility model is to *apply specific tools and techniques* to develop a strategic marketing plan, realigning the organization as necessary to ensure success (Goldman et al. 1995, 280–284). For the manufacturing sector, these strategic planning tools are already in place. Indeed, if you are in industry, all that is necessary is to dial the Agility Forum at 1-800-9BE-AGILE and a consultant will be right with you.

If assistance is not as easily available, the imperatives are there in the not-for-profit sector as well. The topic of Brian Hawkins' recent talk in Dublin, Ohio, was "Creating the Academic Library of the Future: Incrementalism Won't Get Us There." Drawing upon the experience of Brown University, Hawkins suggests that unless paradigms are shifted, libraries will surely fail. We cannot sustain the costs of doing business in the current manner; we cannot keep up with the information spiral.

Reviewing the *agility concepts* for guidance, recall that Goldman and associates posited that effective solutions must incorporate several dimensions:

1. Customers are rewarded with individualized solutions to their needs; they are no longer simply offered a product.
2. The environment is characterized by cooperation, drawing upon strengths to enhance positions in the competitive environment.
3. The organization should set out to master change and conquer uncertainty.
4. The organization must leverage the potential impact of its human and information resources. (Goldman et al. 1995, xv–xvii)

Hawkins' solution to the information explosion and to the soaring costs of information packaged by commercial publishers would be a vast worldwide electronic matrix, a "world mind" to which all parties would be encouraged to contribute in the interest of the general welfare.

This effort, he feels, must come from a new nonprofit corporation which somehow manages to direct the majority of the flow of scientific, medical, and technical publications into a database accessible to all.

Hawkins suggested that higher education should take the initiative to approach Walter Annenberg, who has pledged $500 million to the nation on the behalf of education ("Annenberg" 1993). From the largesse of Mr. Annenberg, a new organization would be formed to formulate a business plan, coordinate the use of existing resources, and receive funds from the many different venues that would be asked to contribute to this "world mind."

Hawkins suggested that librarians, and others in higher education, are at the wrong "unit of analysis" in dealing with the crisis of the Information Revolution. Librarians must not focus their animosities upon the commercial publishers and dwell upon the limitations of our local resources. The agile organization focuses on profitability *tomorrow*. The emphasis is on change, on improvements in costs, time, and quality. Educators should learn to think globally and seek to create a vast information superstructure which would benefit everyone: not just research universities, but all of higher education, K–12, the needs of the corporate community as well as lifelong learning—what he called the "k-to-grey" perspective.

Could it work? Could there emerge a giant, refereed electronic compendium which throws over the whole publish or perish paradigm? Maybe. Rather clearly, the particular initiative relating to the Annenberg largesse has proved fleeting. But at least some downsized version could emerge to serve as one of the avenues by which this new hybrid future is obtained. In the mid-1990s, discussions began between ARL and a presidential committee within the Association of American Universities. One of the task forces has addressed the topic, *A National Strategy for Managing Scientific and Technical Information*. The concern is to create a more competitive and cost-based scholarly publishing environment by enlisting participation of both commercial and not-for-profit organizations. The report emphasized the desirability of retaining in the not-for-profit sector ownership of scientific and technical intellectual property, and suggested the establishment of a national system of electronic depositories for such information ("AAU and ARL" 1994, 4). Those discussions continue and bear promise.

Remember: this is not a race and the initiative does not necessarily rest with the biggest among us. During this time of transition, of movement from one paradigm to the other, the arrow of opportunity may point to smaller, more nimble institutions. The example of the library of Texas Christian University (TCU), which has made a remarkable effort to embrace a new paradigm of scholarship, is offered as an example. As have all research universities with a significant investment in scientific journals, the TCU library has struggled with rising journal costs. Maintenance of its research capability required the doubling of the acquisitions budget over five short years. Much like their counterparts at Brown, TCU planners have been concerned that alternative means be found which satisfy the researcher's needs while slowing the growth curve of the library's materials budget.

To make a long story short, TCU felt that given its strong core collection and the relatively small size of its graduate program, it could substitute "just-in-time" access for some "just-in-case" subscriptions. Rather than cut the journal budget, the campus would fund the transition to a new mode of interaction between library and scholars. One hundred thousand dollars was made available for the acquisition of electronic information in the current budget year. Part of the money was new, and part came from lightly used print journals whose subscriptions were canceled. Faculty, post-doctorates, and graduate students engaged in dissertation research had accounts set up with the vendor of electronic information whose profile most closely matched their research interests. All participants were encouraged to communicate directly from their workstations with the vendors. Current contents review, immediate electronic delivery, and use of standard interlibrary loan were the options available to all. TCU believed that the document delivery fund would make possible a reduction in the number of expensive but little-used titles in the collection. Over-the-horizon projections suggested that by 2003 a mixture of subscriptions and transaction access could mean a savings of as much as $500,000 per annum over the old means of doing business at TCU, wholly within a print environment (Heath 1993).

So there it is. Texas Christian University consciously set about changing its academic culture. Will it work? The jury is still out. Certainly, copyright charges levied by publishers in the document delivery universe are mounting. It may not be a lasting solution. Is the TCU experience transferable? Perhaps not everywhere. Affluence still counts for something, and TCU is certainly one of the wealthier schools in the nation. And size is an issue. What $100,000 can buy for 350 faculty and six Ph.D. programs will cost considerably more at Texas

A&M, where the needs of 3,000 faculty and 80-plus doctoral programs must be addressed. However, elements of the TCU example are being reviewed at Texas A&M, where a considerable investment is now being made to support document delivery and reduce the response time of interlibrary loan.

SUMMARY

Donald Runkle recalls that while lean manufacturing has been codified into a set of 17 principles that his company, General Motors, employs in its manufacturing, the rules of the agile enterprise have not yet been fully compiled. But he knows that they will be developed. "[W]e know that it is important for America to invent the rules for agile manufacturing. We missed the last paradigm shift, and we cannot afford to miss the next one" (Sheridan 1993, 30–46). Without endorsing its precepts specifically, the utility of the agility construct is apparent. The scenario painted by Hawkins in which libraries can prosper in a time of rapid change and the specific example of the TCU response to external forces suggest that the not-for-profit sector can adopt the lessons of the *agile enterprise*.

Robert Holland (1994, 60) explains *agility* concepts using a sailing metaphor:

To successfully sail through the turbulent waters of the twenty-first century, organizations must become fast and agile. In the more stable environment of the past, competition was won by huge battleships like IBM and General Motors, but it is clear that the competitive edge in tomorrow's environment will go to agile organizations with a sure hand at the wheel, an aerodynamic organizational architecture, and quick and finely tuned reflexes.

There is certainly nothing negative in attempting to build an organization that is change proficient, flexibly reconfigurable, and opportunity pulled. Agility is a concept that could serve libraries and the not-for-profit sector well.

REFERENCES

"AAU and ARL Endorse Action Agenda." 1994. *ARL: A Bimonthly Newsletter of Research Library Issues and Actions* (July): 4.

Agility Forum. A web publication. See http://www.agilityforum.org.

"Annenberg to Give Education $500 Million over Five Years." 1993. *New York Times*, December 17, pp. A1, A36.

Burgess, Thomas F. 1994. "Making the Leap to Agility: Defining and Achieving Agile Manufacturing through Business Process Redesign and Business Network Redesign." *International Journal of Operations and Production Management* 14, 11 (November): 23–34.

Cooke, James Aaron. 1995. "Agility Counts." *Traffic Management* 34, 8 (August): 27–31.

Dove, Rick. 1994. "The Meaning of Life and the Meaning of Agile." *Production* 106, 11 (November): 14–15. Also on WWW as: Rick Dove. *The Meaning of Life and the Meaning of Agile.* Purchasing Web. http://www.catalog.com/napmsv/agile.

Everhart, Thomas E. 1993. *Technology and Human Progress: The Information Revolution.* Second Annual Address, The William R. and Evelyn J. Gould Distinguished Lecture on Technology and the Quality of Life, University of Utah, October 7, 1993. [unpaged.]

Goldman, Steven L. 1994. "Agile Competition and Virtual Corporations: The Next American Century." *National Forum: Phi Kappa Phi Journal* 74, 2 (Spring): 43–47.

Goldman, Steven L., Roger N. Nagel, and Kenneth Preiss. 1995. *Agile Competitors and Virtual Organizations: Strategies for Enriching the Customer.* New York: Van Nostrand Reinhold.

Goldman, Steven L., and Kenneth Preiss (eds.); Roger N. Nagel and Rick Dove (principal investigators). 1991. *21st Century Manufacturing Enterprise Strategy.* Vol. 1, *An Industry-led View.* Bethlehem, PA: Iacocca Institute, Lehigh University.

Govan, James F. 1977. "The Better Mousetrap: External Accountability and Staff Participation." *Library Trends* 26 (Fall): 255–268.

Hawkins, Brian. 1994. Vice President for Academic Planning and Administration, Brown University. "Creating the Academic Library of the Future: Incrementalism Won't Get Us There." Paper presented at OCLC Twelfth Annual Conference of Research Library Directors, Dublin, Ohio, March 14–15. (Synopsis derived from my lecture notes.)

Heath, Fred. 1993. "A Leap of Faith: A Campus Moves to Embrace the Electronic Culture." Unpublished manuscript (available from the author). August.

Holland, Robert C. 1994. "Sailing into the Millennium." *Futurist* 28, 1 (January): 60.

Kuhn, Thomas. 1970. *The Structure of Scientific Revolutions.* Chicago: University of Chicago Press.

Max, D. T. 1994. "The End of the Book?" *The Atlantic Monthly* 274, 3 (September): 62–67.

Metrics for the Agile Virtual Enterprise. Executive Overview. The Problem. A web publication at http://www.agilityforum/Ex_Proj/MAVE/12.htm.

Moskal, Brian S. 1995. "Son of Agility." *Industry Week* 244, 10 (May 15): 12–17.

Port, Otis. 1994. "Custom-Made, Direct from the Plant." *Business Week* 3399 (November 18): 158–159.

Port, Otis. 1992. "Moving Past the Assembly Line." *Business Week* (Special Issue: *Reinventing America*): 177–180.

Rogers, David. 1991. *The Bodleian Library and Its Treasures, 1320–1700.* Henley on Thames: Aidan Ellis.

Sheridan, John H. 1993. "Agile Manufacturing: Stepping Beyond Lean Production." *Industry Week* 242, 8 (April 19): 30–46.

Vaisey, David G. 1994. "From Columbus to Computers: Collecting and Accessing a Nation's Cultural Heritage." University Lecture Series, Sterling C. Evans Library and Friends of the Library, Texas A&M University, April 7, 1994. (David Vaisey is Bodley's Librarian, The Bodleian Library, Oxford University.)

Vasilash, Gary S. 1993. "Manufacturing Agility: The Conference." *Production* 105, 4 (April): 58–63.

ANNOTATED BIBLIOGRAPHY

Dimancescu, Dan, and Kemp Dwenger. 1996. *World-class New Product Development: Benchmarking Best Practices of Agile Manufactures.* New York: AMACOM. The focus of this book is to identify and show the importance of communication throughout the organization when developing a product. The book is divided into two parts. The first part covers the theory behind creating an organization where all levels of an organization are brought together in teams to create a new product. These teams help to reduce waste efforts and product development time by making the group responsible for the product from concept to production. The second part of the book uses case studies to illustrate points from the first part. While libraries do not have the same type of "product development" as industries, this book raises some interesting points, such as surveying the customer before development and doing follow-through after delivery of a product.

Dove, Rick, 1994. "The Meaning of Life and the Meaning of Agile." *Production* 106, 11 (November): 14–15. Also available as a web publication (http://www. catalog.com/napmsv/agile). In this brief article Rick Dove states that agility is the "missing characteristic" of organizations who use lean manufacturing, TQM, and mass customization. He contends that an organization which is agile can quickly respond to changes in its environment, thus fulfilling a need and maintaining its existence until the change occurs. This article clarifies what agility is in terms of organization. For librarians, the article is helpful to grasp the basic definition and concept of organizational agility.

Goldman, Steven L., Roger N. Nagel, and Kenneth Preiss. 1995. *Agile Competitors and Virtual Organizations: Strategies for Enriching the Customer.* New York: Van Nostrand Reinhold. This book focuses on the concept of agile competition as processing capability to treat the masses as individuals. It examines the reasons why agility is a solution for companies to stay competitive and profitable. The challenges facing libraries can be found in the industry-based examples, in particular the challenge of responding to a growing demand by customers for value-added services and not just physical products. There are several interesting ideas, among them the idea of a virtual company made up of working with an Internet search engine company to create individualized patron profiles for searching and identifying appropriate web sites. The authors of this book are leading thinkers in agility and were among the facilitators at Lee Iacocca's first Agility Institute and have participated in Iacocca's Agility Forum.

Goldman, Steven L., and Kenneth Preiss (eds.); Roger N. Nagel and Rick Dove (principal investigators). 1991. *21st Century Manufacturing Enterprise Strategy.* Bethlehem, PA: Iacocca Institute, Lehigh University. This two-volume report is the result of a study conducted by a consortium of leading representatives from industry, government, and academia. Volume 1 (*An Industry-led View*) and volume 2 (*Infrastructure*) led to a vision of what the world of manufacturing will be like in the year 2006, as well as an analysis of the infrastructure needed to support that vision.

Maskell, Brian H. 1994. *Software and the Agile Manufacturer: Computer Systems and World Class Manufacturing*. Portland, OR: Productivity Press. The author states in the preface that leadership and management can achieve agility. Computers and computer software can help them in the transition. He also states that current computer systems and software were developed to support traditional manufacturing systems. Agility requires simple and "easy to use" systems. Throughout the book he uses examples of how actual companies have begun to make the transition using computers and computer software to help them. Librarians will find the book helpful as they begin to modify existing computer systems that were developed to support proprietary systems and software.

Preiss, Kenneth. 1995. *Mass, Lean, and Agile as Static and Dynamic Systems*. Bethlehem, PA: Agile Manufacturing Enterprise Forum. This work leads to a deeper understanding of mass, lean, and agile systems and their operating criteria by comparing a business system to a structural beam. It is suggested that mass, lean, and agile systems be viewed as static, decoupled; static, coupled; and dynamic, coupled systems. This in turn leads to a better understanding of the behavior and design of the total value-adding chain for these modes of operation.

2

Managing Change

Rebecca R. Martin

THE CHALLENGE

Rapid, far-reaching change is emerging as the dominant paradigm for entering the twenty-first century. Whether the focus is models for industry, for government, or for information, the common theme is change. Rosabeth Moss Kanter and her colleagues (1992) assert that in the coming decade, responding to change, harnessing change, and creating change will become the major challenges facing organizations. The organizations that survive will be those that view change as an opportunity rather than a threat. It is essential that the university library capitalize upon this environment of change in order to maintain the central role in campus programs which it has held for many years. To create the agile library, library organizational structures, staff roles, and fundamental goals will need to be reworked. Recent authors have disagreed about whether or not this change will require revolution (Stoffle et al. 1996) or reorientation (Lee 1996), but it is clear that radical change will be required. It is likely that by the end of this decade, every job within the academic library will have undergone significant change when compared with assignments of the recent past or the present. Organizational relationships will depart from the familiar hierarchy, and the focus of library operations will shift to meet new user demands. Change of this magnitude is never easy, and it will present significant challenges to individuals at all levels of the organization.

In considering the restructuring of a major university library, James G. Neal and Patricia A. Steele (1993) identified 27 key principles and assumptions which provide the foundation for such redefinition; nine of these are particularly salient in relation to the issues of managing change:

- Administrative responsibility and authority must be distributed more widely throughout the organization.
- Flexibility in structure is essential to organizational health and vitality.
- Work is increasingly accomplished through project teams.
- The evolving work environment will involve expanding overlap and ambiguity among the responsibilities of different employee groups.
- Innovation must be encouraged by the structures . . . and reward systems of the library.
- Small-group collaboration is essential.
- The personal productivity of individual employees must receive expanded attention.
- More resources and staff time must be allocated to staff and professional development.
- Library administrators must take a more critical approach to current operations and programs.

The challenge in redefining libraries along these lines will encompass new roles for leaders, greater empowerment for staff, and altered organizational structures. In the following pages, these issues will be addressed in terms of both theoretical perspectives and practical approaches.

LEADERSHIP FOR CHANGE

A conventional point to begin a discussion of organizational change is with the role of the leader. In the complex environment facing universities and libraries, managing change has become a critical component of leadership. Peter F. Drucker (1975, 79) states that "for managers, the dynamics of knowledge impose one clear imperative: every organization has to build the management of change into its very structure." The stable, rule-oriented structures of traditional organizations must give way to more fluid forms capable of responding to new demands. As Susan Lee (1993) points out, management's focus should be on designing and bringing into being the institutional processes through which new problems can continually be confronted and old structures continually discarded.

This focus on change puts new demands on library managers, who must plan for the future while dealing with the daily operations of the library. To be effective, these managers must have a good understanding of where they are as well as where they want to go (Faerman 1993). Building consensus around a vision of the future which makes sense within the context of the present may be the most important component in leading this change. For example, as we move to a user-centered library, individuals who have devoted their careers to building collections and bibliographic access systems must be able to see their contributions in the context of the new library vision in a way which enables them to continue to be productive members of the organization.

The agile library organization of the immediate future calls for flexibility and adaptability in those individuals who lead them. In order to guide a library through the transition process demanded by the changing environment, a pivotal skill for library leaders is the capacity to deal with uncertainty without losing sight of the vision. Lee (1994, 22) identifies the need for cognitive complexity, stating that:

Effective leaders know the direction in which they are headed. Their organization's strategic vision provides the compass but not the road map. . . . The cognitively complex executive is the flexible thinker, making decisions on the run, decisions that are based on, and revised because of, new information.

Persistence in pursuing the vision is critical, although the methods chosen may need to be flexible.

Sue R. Faerman (1993) identifies eight roles for library leaders initiating change, based on different models of organizational theory: innovator, broker, director, producer, coordinator, monitor, mentor, and facilitator. In performing these roles or a combination thereof, library leaders approach managing the transition of a changing library in different ways, emphasizing varying components of the change process.

In focusing on the external environment, the leader may serve as an innovator or a broker. The innovator is concerned with the organization's adaptability and readiness to cope with changes. As innovators, leaders create the vision for change which defines the future direction of the organization and help others within the organization to adapt to change. Creative thinking and an ability to see problems as opportunities are important in this role. As broker, the leader serves as a liaison between the library and those outside, communicating with others about the work of the organization, and ensuring that the organization's image remains positive. Negotiation for resources in the shifting environment is a primary activity.

Another approach emphasizes organizational effectiveness, with the leader taking the role of director or producer. To enhance organizational effectiveness, the leader as director develops organizational plans for the future, provides direction for others, and clarifies expectations about the organization's mission and goals. Strategic planning and goal setting, common in many academic library change efforts described in the literature (Neal and Steele 1993; Storey 1995, for example), would fall into this leadership role. In addition to developing the plan, the leader must also ensure that employees understand the organizational vision and plan, are committed to this vision, and see their own individual roles in carrying out the plan. As producer, the leader emphasizes productivity and accomplishment in the implementation of the new plan.

Also related to organizational effectiveness is an approach which focuses on internal processes. As library organizations move toward models which expand employees' responsibilities and discretion, leadership roles of coordinator and monitor may be appropriate. In the monitor role, leaders emphasize communication and information management, critical elements for effectiveness in a turbulent and changing organization environment. For example, the ability to make a transition to a more user-centered organization requires a library to gather, analyze, and interpret data on user needs in new ways; in some cases these activities have become a focal point for the process of organizational change. In another process role, that of coordinator, the leader uses reorganization and management of assignments to change the structure and flow of the organizational system to meet new needs.

Finally, a focus on human relations and the importance of employees as valued resources within the organization generate roles for the leader as mentor and facilitator. In the mentor role, leaders are concerned with the management of individual resources and are sensitive to the need to treat each person as an individual. In organizations where all staff roles are undergoing significant change, this is a critical and time-consuming component of leadership. Staff training, career development, and individual counseling are prominent. A related role is that of facilitator, which is concerned with group interactions and performance. Building cohesion in groups, managing conflict, and negotiating compromise are important leadership activities in organizations moving toward collectively-based work structures.

In developing these descriptions of roles for library leaders in changing organizations, Faerman (1993) acknowledges that while leaders may favor a particular approach based on their organizational setting and management style, there is a need for balance among these functions, all of which need to be addressed at some point in an organization in transition. Too much emphasis on any one role may lead to a negative result, and a combination of strategies may be most useful in leading a library through organizational change.

Leadership may also come from various parts of the organization, with managers working in different capacities assuming some of these roles. With a complementary team approach, a group of library administrators may be able to effectively meet the need for leadership along these different dimensions.

Regardless of the approach taken to leadership in the change process, a critical component in the effectiveness of the leader is the relationship between the leader and those she or he hopes to lead. In his analysis of organizations undergoing profound change, James O'Toole (1995, 37) described the importance of this relationship in very compelling terms:

Leaders fail when they have an inappropriate attitude and philosophy about the relationship between themselves and their followers. Those who do not respect and trust their followers cannot lead them. Conversely, those who succeed at bringing about effective and moral change believe in and act on the inherent dignity of those they lead, in particular, in their natural, human capacity to reason. In bringing about change, these leaders of leaders always include the people affected in the change process. Hence, wherever successful leaders may start the process, whatever particular program they may adopt, and however they may choose to proceed along the way, they always practice the art of inclusion.

While it is hard to escape O'Toole's message on the importance of involvement throughout the organization in bringing about organizational change, it is not a point that can be overemphasized here. Carla J. Stoffle (Stoffle et al. 1996, 220) observes that "the most fundamental change that has to occur among library employees is a switch from a focus on things and organizing library work around things to a focus on customers and their needs." If that is the case, then the employees themselves must be actively involved in redefining the library organization, or their focus will remain on the status quo.

STAFF EMPOWERMENT

The assumptions with which this chapter began, indeed Fred Heath's model in Chapter 1 for the agile library itself, call for a library organization in which all members play a substantive role in problem solving and decision making, both in relation to daily tasks and in planning for a future of change.

The movement toward greater empowerment for staff, a dominant theme in management literature, has recently become a feature of models for new organizational structures in academic libraries. The increasing complexity of work throughout libraries, due in part to the prevalence of automated systems, requires decision making at the lowest levels. Detailed expertise and experience rest with the staff and fewer decisions are referred to the manager for approval. However, it is important to recognize that staff empowerment goes beyond the more familiar participative management, requiring a long-term perspective, persistence, and a strong commitment to individual and organizational development (von Dran 1993).

The role of leadership in staff empowerment is critical, as the shift toward this orientation demands nothing short of transformation of the organization's culture. Leaders must begin from the belief that staff are capable members of the organization who are committed to its success. They need to encourage a shared leadership in which staff assume a mutual responsibility for high performance, at both the individual and the organizational levels (Sullivan 1991).

Maureen Sullivan (1991) identifies the following strategies for moving a traditional library organization to one which stresses developing high performance and empowering staff:

- Develop teams
- Train and develop staff for now and the future
- Plan and assess performance

- Lead by example
- Analyze current patterns of work and redesign jobs
- Define career paths
- Manage ambiguity
- Hire the best possible staff
- Review personnel policies and systems
- Reward success, acknowledge achievement, and praise effort
- Attend to your own development

While many of these may appear to be ordinary activities for a library manager, they are pursued in this context with a goal of developing new relationships, organizational structures, and work behaviors which focus on self-responsibility and shared responsibility. Problems are seen as opportunities for both the staff and the leaders to learn and develop their skills and activities, moving from a dependent relationship to one of interdependence.

The movement from traditional managerial roles and structures to strategies based on greater involvement and empowerment of staff will create stress throughout the organization. As Gisela M. von Dran (1993, 14) states,

Employing empowerment strategies will upset the organizational equilibrium and threaten the comfort zones of those unwilling to change. Old expectations, assumptions, and ways of doing things will be challenged and conflict will increase. Employees who were comfortable with and worked well under traditional expectations may react negatively to the new responsibilities, risks, and time requirements of participation and decision making. The more diverse the work force, the higher the level of conflict which is to be expected.

As these obstacles are overcome, the change, though destabilizing, will also be energizing for the organization and its members.

Thomas W. Shaughnessy (1996) makes some astute observations regarding his experiences with reorganization and staff empowerment in a major research library. In this case, planning for library restructuring was put entirely in the hands of the staff, with little involvement from top administration. Interestingly, the large group of staff involved in the open restructuring effort encountered reactions of skepticism and mistrust, usually reserved for administrators, from those within the library who were committed to the status quo. The process took more time than was expected and in some ways became an end unto itself. Managers experienced difficulties in letting go of command and control. Most importantly, Shaughnessy found the wisdom of the library staff throughout this effort to be extraordinary, resulting in a reorganized library system which is more nimble, team directed, and responsive.

As libraries confront the changing environment which demands adaptation and flexibility in order to meet new needs, a critical resource to be considered rests within the staff. Empowering all of the people engaged in running libraries and providing services to users in the transition process is an important step in the success of the organizational change.

THE PROCESS OF RESTRUCTURING

The significant changes occurring in academic libraries have been characterized by some as fundamental organizational transformation. Shelley E. Phipps (1993, 19) captures the essence of this transformation in a concrete way, stating that libraries

are being transformed from collection centered organizations to access organizations; from repositories of the printed format to organizations that are less tied to place, to paper, and to print. They are linking users to information held locally or available remotely, and are empowering users to become self-sufficient information finders . . . the roles played by the library in the scholarly communication process are becoming more proactive, assertive, and collaborative.

Organizational change in support of this transformation is taking many forms, and most often managers in complex organizations are likely to face the prospect of working within several types of organizational structures.

Approaches to restructuring academic libraries have taken different forms, some adopting techniques developed in private sector organizations such as team-based management, learning organizations, matrix management, and Total Quality Management. Others have employed modifications on such themes to develop designs unique to their individual settings. Examples of these strategies are well documented in the library management literature and provide a good starting point for the preliminary consideration of reorganization possibilities.[1]

The way in which an organization is restructured, redesigned, or reduced affects all of its members. Although organizational change is often viewed from the perspective of the leader or manager, the process is influenced by all of those involved. Understanding the components of this process can add to the success of the change effort.

In considering restructuring at the university level, Alan E. Guskin (1996) contends that the most important and perhaps most difficult step is beginning the process of change. There are many reasons to put off the hard work of organizational change, including the inherent pain and difficulties, but the turmoil in the environment will force changes eventually. Although his observations were made at the broader institutional level, they hold relevance for academic libraries as well. He found that any restructuring effort requires the development of a working consensus on the urgent need to restructure and on the vision of the institution's future. In conducting the change process, the leadership should seek out those people who are supportive of the change effort and work with them. Finally, he notes that the restructured institution does not emerge whole at one time; rather, it is implemented in a series of phases that evolve over time.

Patrick E. Connor and Linda K. Lake (1994) propose a model for conducting a change effort which has four major components. The first segment is composed of the initiating processes, including acknowledgment of the destabilizing forces, analysis of the organization against standards or models, formulation of a problem statement, and development of proposed solutions. In the second phase, participants determine whether the ideal solution can be implemented. This envisioning includes the description of the current and future organizational states, assessment of the differences between them, and identification of restraining and facilitating factors.

In the third segment of the change model, actual plans for carrying out the change are crafted. At this point, the vision is revised, a transition profile is constructed, and strategies and tactics for the change are developed. In the final stage, the changes are implemented, institutionalized, and evaluated. While this theoretical model of the process may not adequately reflect the fluid nature of organizational change as it is experienced in libraries, it is helpful to analyze the various stages which are entailed.

Unfortunately, many libraries are undergoing reductions in size at the same time that restructuring is taking place. Cameron et al. (1993) studied 30 organizations to uncover the best practices in organizations attempting to downsize and increase organizational effectiveness. Three types of implementation strategies were observed, often used in combination. The first of these is *work force reduction*, where the number of employees in the work force is simply decreased, often through attrition. Many academic libraries have experienced this type of change. Another strategy is *organizational redesign*, where functions, hierarchical levels, groups or divisions are eliminated, tasks are redesigned, and units are consolidated. This is a common approach in academic libraries making conscious organizational changes. Finally, the authors described *systemic change*, where the organization's culture and the attitudes and values of employees are changed over a long-term period. Systemic change is more unusual in libraries; however, it may be early to assess evidence of such change in current reorganization efforts.

Organizations often use these strategies in combination. How organizations implement these strategies can also make a difference. Factors that positively affect organizational improvement during downsizing include systematic analysis of tasks and personnel in advance, gradual, incremental implementation of changes, increased communication and participation, and increased employee effort. Factors that lead to organizational deterioration during downsizing include downsizing via attrition, more work required for remaining employees, alterations in the reward and appraisal systems, and no improvement in quality. The best downsizing practices were characterized by total organizational effort in improving performance, participation in downsizing endeavors, downsizing viewed as an opportunity, and individuals defined as resources to foster organizational improvement.

TRANSITION AND THE INDIVIDUAL

Finally, the change process must also be considered at the individual level. As the organization undergoes significant change, the individuals involved must adapt and adjust to new circumstances. Librarians and library staff are under significant pressure to embrace new roles in their libraries and universities. However, given resource constraints in most institutions, demand for new roles will not generate new positions. This means that people need to find ways to change how they view and perform their work to meet changing demands.

Much of the literature on the changes in society identifies knowledge workers as principal players in the emerging paradigm. The description of knowledge workers as team oriented, interdisciplinary, able to handle greater role complexity, and comfortable with looser lines of authority closely parallels the roles for library staff in the new organization models discussed above. However, this is not necessarily an easy transition for people who entered libraries to perform work in which they would be working independently, focused on specialized areas, and engaged in detailed and rule-oriented tasks with clear job expectations.

As the lines between professional and paraprofessional assignments blur, uncertainty regarding appropriate roles occurs. Issues of background and expertise, decision making, status, and self-identity are raised. Transition to new definitions of organizational roles may require individuals to refocus their expectations of their jobs and even their careers.

In addition, assumptions that people always want more information and more decision-making responsibilities may be inaccurate. Some leaders in team-based management organizations observe that more access to information does not mean that staff will be able to deal with more information. Loss of the management filter means that people at all levels need to be more involved in thinking about major organizational issues. Some staff thrive in this situation but for others, too much information and uncertainty leads to a loss of control (Stoffle 1994).

These new roles carry many new demands, including new skills, added workload, changed expectations, and in some cases, transformed career paths. An important concern in understanding acceptance of change at the individual level is the critical nature of time. Major organizational change can be similar to a major life change in the impact that it has on each individual. Change of this magnitude requires time to be understood, time to be accepted, and time to be embraced. Unlike the situation faced by one person in entering a new job, in a changing organization, often everyone in a unit has a new role and is experiencing the stress of change. People need time to adjust to what they should view as entirely new jobs, even if they are sitting at the same desks.

Many staff members will experience these changes as a threat to their job security. While job design undergoes major transformation, the assumption that one may continue in the same position for many years to come may be unrealistic. Elimination of positions through downsizing in the library or elsewhere in the institution can serve to heighten perceptions that a secure job is no longer a reasonable expectation. At the same time, most individuals working in libraries have considerable expertise that will be valuable in a new function or in roles which are related to their previous assignments. A commitment to maintaining a viable place for each individual in the library, through reassignment, training, and development, can help make what has been called employability security an important element in new organizational relationships.

Judy Clarke (1995) encourages library managers to create an environment for people to make the transition to new roles and altered organizational structures. She asserts that intellectual and emotional acceptance of change is as important as the physical acceptance characterized by the undertaking of new tasks or the move to a different office. She proposes several steps for individuals managing a transition which are modified here for use by library managers:

- Accept and expect that during the time your staff experience change, they will experience feelings of loss.
- Build and maintain support systems for everyone involved.
- Encourage people to take care of themselves physically.
- Honor the past as a tactic in surviving the transition.
- Help staff inventory their assets and strengths rather than focus on their inadequacies.
- Create a ritual or ceremony to facilitate the process of letting go.
- Begin to create a picture of the future and a new beginning.
- Identify fears and make plans for confronting them.
- Recognize and build on risk-taking behavior.
- Encourage people to identify what they want and to set priorities.
- Help everyone view change as an opportunity to grow, to learn, and to self-renew.

Understanding and attending to the human side of organizational change will strengthen the management of the change process.

ORGANIZATIONAL RESISTANCE

Resistance to organizational change is an evitable part of the change process, one which must be understood if it is to be overcome. O'Toole (1995, 248) explores this issue in depth and concludes that people are often likely to resist change, even when it is in their interest, for the following reasons:

- Resistance to change occurs when a would-be leader challenges the comfort of the group, the members' satisfaction with the established level of their power, prestige, privileges, position, and satisfaction with who they are, what they believe, and what they cherish.

- Individuals are what they believe, and groups are their cultures; hence to require a group to change its shared beliefs is to threaten its very existence . . . Peaceful change thus requires acquiescence in upsetting the dominant world view . . . in effect, the collective eating of crow by those who have the power to resist change.

- In almost all instances, the majority of people who have power resist the call to reform not so much because they fear change, but because they bristle at having the will of others imposed on them. . . . Thus a major factor in our resistance to change is the desire not to have the will of others forced upon us.

In considering the application of these ideas to academic libraries, it is important to recognize that the power to resist change exists at all levels of the organization, as the acceptance of new modes of operation will be necessary by all involved for the change to be successful.

In an important book entitled *Overcoming Organizational Defenses*, Chris Argyris (1990) asserts that when individuals feel threatened or embarrassed, as is often the case when confronted by major change, they are likely to engage in defensive reasoning. Understanding the dynamics of this defensiveness can help managers avoid these obstacles or at least build bridges around them. He paints some vivid pictures of the potential consequences of this defensiveness in organizations undergoing change:

1. Actions intended to increase understanding and trust often produce misunderstanding and mistrust. For example, a manager leaves a meeting where change has been discussed believing that full agreement has been reached, but later commitments are not met and change does not occur. Or, participatory meetings on tough issues occur, but hard questions cannot be addressed, leaving people confused as to the outcome.

2. Individuals may protect themselves by blaming the system or others for prior decisions. When major problems occur, some people may fall back on the old excuse of just following rules and procedures and avoid making change.

3. The tried and proven ways of doing things dominate organizational life, leading to organizational inertia. Some may engage in creating apparent movement to assure others that actions are being taken, while buying time to figure out how to avoid change altogether. Idea breakers, such as "I don't have the authority," "the director won't like it," and "we just don't do it that way" can be very powerful.

4. Upward communications for difficult issues are often lacking. Fearing that the messenger may bear the flow for the message, middle managers may fail to pass along information about negative attitudes, expectations, or service problems. This fails to show proper respect for front-line employees and a lack of adequate understanding of the process necessary for change. Everyone loses.

5. Budget games are necessary evils. These are a fact of life in organizations and may be used effectively to block change. Managers may attempt to support budgetary requests which maintain the status quo with voluminous data for which the relevance is not clear, or argue that the real benefit of the service or operation is subjective. This type of game playing should not be rewarded.

6. People do not behave reasonably, even when it is in their best interest. When faced with upsetting facts, people may react in unpredictable ways. Behaviors such as procrastination, indecision, lack of follow-up, rejection, and even sabotage may occur when people threatened by change try to protect themselves.

Argyris notes that although they are widespread, these harmful defensive tactics need not be inevitable, and where they are found they can be turned around. Managers who are aware of these defensive mechanisms in themselves and in their staffs may provide the key to finding the solution and moving forward.

After taking these factors into account, it is also important for the leader to question whether or not the resistance is based upon substantive concerns with how the proposed change will work. The engagement of the entire staff in the process of organizational change will inevitably lead to disagreement about appropriate courses of action, even when the capacity for change and a strong commitment to a forward-looking agenda exist.

Stress may come from what Peter M. Senge (1990) calls creative tension, resulting from the gap between vision and current reality. He uses the metaphor of a rubber band stretched between these two points, either pulling current reality toward the vision or holding the vision back because of the forces of the present. While libraries attempt to organize to make innovative strides toward new roles and services, the current demands of library programs and operations form the daily reality. In keeping with Senge's metaphor of a rubber band, all involved must work to ensure that the creative tension moves the current reality toward the vision, rather than allowing the present pressures to hold it back.

ETHICAL ISSUES

Before concluding this discussion of managing change, it is important to raise some ethical questions which should be considered by every leader initiating a change effort. Matters of individual employment and careers are at stake, and the manner in which these are handled can have serious implications for the entire organization. These concerns may be complicated in some cases by collective bargaining agreements, but are of consequence in all institutional settings.

Connor and Lake (1994) cast these questions in the context of three areas of justice. Since organizational change often involves the redistribution of resources, the issue of distributive justice must be addressed. Leaders should question, was the redistribution performed fairly, that is, equitably, equally, and in accordance with people's needs? Secondly, procedural justice is required, prompting the questions of whether the various parties to the change had sufficient voice in the matter and whether valid systems of challenge or recourse were provided. Finally, in the area of interactional justice, did management deal with employees justly, by honestly giving explanations of why change is needed, why certain target groups and strategies were selected, and what outcomes were likely to occur?

With thought, care, and respect for everyone involved in the change process, these ethical issues can be handled effectively and the restructuring can proceed.

CONCLUSION

Change has become a way of life in academic libraries. The shifting paradigm of higher education and the escalating evolution of information technology are likely to bring about even greater change in our organizations to become dynamic, proactive, adaptable, and creative in response to our changing environment is a significant undertaking. Meeting this challenge is one key to the viability of our libraries and the future of our institutions.

NOTE

1. See, for example, Phipps 1993; Storey 1995; Neal and Steele 1993; Shaughnessy 1996; Schwartz 1997; Riggs 1993.

REFERENCES

Argyris, Chris. 1990. *Overcoming Organizational Defenses*. Boston: Allyn and Bacon.

Cameron, Kim S., Sarah J. Freeman, and Aneil K. Mishra. 1993. "Downsizing and Redesigning Organizations." In G. Huber and W. Glick (eds.), *Organizational Change and Redesign* (pp. 19–63). New York: Oxford University Press.

Clarke, Judy. 1995. "Understanding Transition: The People Side of Managing Change." *Serials Librarian* 25: 193–202.

Connor, Patrick E., and Linda K. Lake. 1994. *Managing Organizational Change*, 2nd ed. Westport, Conn.: Praeger.

Drucker, Peter F. 1995. *Managing in a Time of Great Change*. New York: Truman Talley Books/Dutton.

Faerman, Sue R. 1993. "Organizational Change and Leadership Styles." *Journal of Library Administration* 19: 55–79.

Guskin, Alan E. 1996. "Facing the Future: The Change Process in Restructuring Universities." *Change* 28: 27–37.

Kanter, Rosabeth Moss, Barry A. Stein, and Todd D. Jick. 1992. *The Challenge of Organizational Change*. New York: The Free Press.

Lee, Susan. 1996. "Change: But Not So Fast and Not So Much." *College and Research Libraries* 57: 226–228.

———. 1994. "Leadership: Revised and Redesigned for the Electronic Age." *Journal of Library Administration* 20: 17–28.

———. 1993. "Organizational Change in Research Libraries." *Journal of Library Administration* 18: 129–143.

Neal, James G., and Patricia A. Steele. 1993. "Empowerment, Organization and Struc-
    ture." *Journal of Library Administration* 19: 81–96.
O'Toole, James. 1995. *Leading Change: Overcoming the Ideology of Comfort and the
    Tyranny of Custom.* San Francisco: Jossey-Bass.
Phipps, Shelley E. 1993. "Transforming Libraries into Learning Organizations—The
    Challenge for Leadership." *Journal of Library Administration* 18: 19–37.
Riggs, Donald E. 1993. "Managing Quality: TQM in Libraries." *Library Administration
    and Management* 7: 73–79.
Schwartz, Charles A., ed. 1997. *Restructuring the Academic Library in the Wake of
    Technological Change.* Chicago: Association of College and Research Libraries.
Senge, Peter M. 1990. *The Fifth Discipline: The Art and Practice of the Learning Or-
    ganization.* New York: Doubleday.
Shaughnessy, Thomas W. 1996. "Lessons from Restructuring the Library." *Journal of
    Academic Librarianship* 22: 251–256.
Stoffle, Carla J. 1994. "Connections: Working in the Networked Organization." Paper
    read at the Coalition for Networked Information, Orlando, Fla.
Stoffle, Carla J., Robert Renaud, and Jerilyn R. Veldof. 1996. "Choosing Our Futures."
    College and Research Libraries 57: 213–233.
Storey, Colin. 1995. "The Impact of Information Technology on Management and Or-
    ganization: The Case of Hong Kong Polytechnic University Library." *Library
    Management* 16: 23–33.
Sullivan, Maureen. 1991. "A New Leadership Paradigm: Empowering Library Staff and
    Improving Performance." *Journal of Library Administration* 14: 73–85.
von Dran, Gisela M. 1993. "Empowerment—A Strategy for Change." *Journal of Li-
    brary Administration* 18: 3–18.

ANNOTATED BIBLIOGRAPHY

Argyris, Chris. 1990. *Overcoming Organizational Defenses.* Boston: Allyn and Bacon.
    Organizational behavior during periods of turmoil and change takes defensive
    forms as people feel threatened. Perceiving the dynamics of defensive reasoning
    is a key to overcoming organizational resistance, and specific tactics and ap-
    proaches are outlined here.
Clarke, Judy. 1995. "Understanding Transition: The People Side of Managing Change."
    Serials Librarian 25: 193–202. Understanding the human side of organizational
    change is critical to managing the continuous change confronting libraries as they
    approach the twenty-first century. This article covers the difficulties people have
    coping with change and the importance of the transition process.
Connor, Patrick E., and Linda K. Lake. 1994. *Managing Organizational Change,* 2nd
    ed. Westport, Conn.: Praeger. Specific techniques and processes for managing
    change are presented in this handbook, which views organizations as human in-
    struments and management as the art and science of exercising options.
Lee, Susan. 1993. "Organizational Change in Research Libraries." *Journal of Library
    Administration* 18: 129–143. Taking a political perspective of the change process,
    Lee asserts that strategic organizational change should replace strategic planning
    as the appropriate response from library leaders in today's environment. Training

for behavioral competence and building flexible organizational units must take place in a fluid context for research libraries to flourish and succeed.

Phipps, Shelley E. 1993. "Transforming Libraries into Learning Organizations—The Challenge for Leadership." *Journal of Library Administration* 18: 19–37. Peter Senge's model of the learning organization is explained and applied to academic libraries, with particular emphasis on empowering staff and developing new roles for leaders.

Senge, Peter M. 1990. *The Fifth Discipline: The Art and Practice of the Learning Organization.* New York: Doubleday. Organizations that excel in the future will be those that are based on people's commitment and capacity to learn at all levels of the organization. This important book addresses the need to transform institutions into learning organizations, creating a new paradigm based upon systems thinking, personal mastery, mental models, shared vision, and team learning.

Shaughnessy, Thomas W. 1996. "Lessons from Restructuring the Library." *Journal of Academic Librarianship* 22: 251–256. Reorganization processes at the University of Minnesota Libraries are described, with an emphasis on the work of staff design and implementation teams. Anticipated and unexpected issues emerging from the restructuring are explored, providing thoughtful observations on organizational change experiences in a large university library.

Sullivan, Maureen. 1991. "A New Leadership Paradigm: Empowering Library Staff and Improving Performance." *Journal of Library Administration* 14: 73–85. Empowerment and meaningful involvement of staff at all levels of the organization are critical steps to improved organizational performance. A new paradigm for leadership is described, including strategies for library managers to consider as they increase the role of staff in library problem solving and decision making.

3

The Technologically Agile Library

T. J. Lusher

INTRODUCTION

Every revolution has a symbol. The liberty tree during the American Revolutionary War and World War II's Rosie the Riveter are examples of long-lasting symbols of the revolutions they represented. For the telecommunication and information revolution, the Internet-connected computer with a user sitting at the computer exploring the World Wide Web is becoming a very powerful symbol for American society, with our historical fascination with technology, from Jefferson's agricultural experiments to the Apollo 13 landing. The user-and-computer symbol represents freedom of information and the information seekers' independence from reliance on the traditional workplace and research centers.

For libraries, this symbol represents both the exciting new territory of information work and the demise of traditional librarianship. To survive the revolution, libraries and librarians must learn how to be technologically agile.

In Chapter 1 of this book, Fred Heath describes agility as a mind-set that allows the organization to respond quickly to changing patron expectations. How can a library, with its banks of computers and peripherals, miles of hard wire, and small equipment budgets, be agile? The library begins to travel the road to agility by studying its existing information technology structure.

Suppose you were asked to engage in one of those memory games that always points out how little attention we all pay to details. Could you describe the arrangement of your office—not of the clutter on your desk or your hard drive, but the equipment itself? Where is your computer in relation to the telephone? Now, attempt to describe your library. How many public workstations are there, and where are they placed? How many staff have computers on their desks, and are the staff computers appropriate for the staff's tasks? Where are and how many etherwave connections does the library have? Which platform and in what format do the library's electronic resources run? How many different ways can you access a resource? To quote a freshman, "Where's the InfoTrac?" You work there, some may accuse you of living there, but still it proves hard to describe the technology in a library from memory. It seems, however, that this is the way many libraries are planning their futures, what they will consist of, what they will become.

If the library staff and administration of the University of XYZ were building a new library, they would certainly have a plan to discover how the library was going to be used by its patrons. Also, staff and administration would communicate their needs and wants to the architect who would draw up floor plans to reflect, it is hoped, the needs and wants and hypothetical uses of all the library users and staff. It would be an exciting, proactive, *planful* process.

For most library administrators and staff, the opportunity to design a new building will not present itself, and we must build our new libraries within the walls of old structures, requiring the old library to respond with agility. Agility enables the library to be flexible, to re-envision itself, to become able to meet the changing demands of its patrons as quickly as those demands become known.

Throughout this book, the authors examine the impact of technology on students and library staff and how technology changes or reinvents how the library is marketed, ensuring that the library is providing the patron with a positive experience. The theories and insights shared by this book's authors provide the framework for our needs and wants for the future library.[1]

Where do we start to build the agile library? In *Technology, Management, and Society* (1970, 131), Drucker asked, "what do we have to do today to be ready for an uncertain tomorrow?" One way the agile library can become ready is in preparing a "topological technology map" showing the smallest of detail about the information technology infrastructure of the existing library. This is not a new concept, for it is based on the spreadsheet/database inventory methods many libraries already use to track their equipment. The difference is in the presentation of information. For example, an inventory database is one-dimensional; to use it you have to look at a long row of information for each item. A topological technology map provides a visual, two-dimensional representation of the same information, but symbols or color in addition to text helps represent the information. This topological map is an easy-to-prepare, practical tool which libraries may use to begin to prepare today for tomorrow, to provide a bridge between theory and reality.[2]

TECHNOLOGY MAPS

Topological Technology Map

The general purpose of the library information technology map is to give an overall understanding of the information technology structure of the library, but more importantly, the topological technology map will help the library administrator plot the course for new information technology adoption. For example, the Libraries of the University of Luddite (LUL), a medium-sized, midwestern university, are planning a major technology upgrade. This upgrade will include purchasing of new computers for the staff and public areas, launching a digitization project, and placing the library's numerous stand-alone electronic databases on a local area network available through the campus backbone. Additionally, the consortium CONE (the Coalition Organization to Network Everything), of which LUL is a member, will be converting to a Web-based automation system in six months. For LUL, the topological map will show where the staff and public computers are currently located, and where the data lines and electrical outlets can be found. It will also show the format, platform, and access channel of the electronic resources. The computer, data lines, and electrical outlet information will be overlaid by the format, platform, and access map. The map makes it easy to quickly see where the technology ''gaps'' exist. Taken as a multidimensional descriptive tool, the map positions the library to make intelligent selections about new technology, and how the new technology will change staff responsibilities, and the products the library has to offer.[3]

The First Layer of the Topological Technology Map: Computers, Data Lines, and Electrical Outlets

The first layer of the map will illustrate, in scale, computer equipment, data, and electrical outlet locations (see Figure 1) of a given floor of LUL's main library. This layer of the map will enable the LUL administration and staff to know what computer equipment and peripherals the library currently owns—for example, the number of computers, their processing levels, and where the equipment is located. The map can be developed to note any attributes of the equipment a library administrator deems important, symbolically, graphically, or in text, such as age of the equipment, whether or not the equipment can be upgraded, and the level of computing power available to staff and faculty. This information will help the LUL systems office to identify areas of greatest need when installing the first round of new computers.

In addition, the library servers need to be described in some detail (i.e., processing speed, RAM, hard drive size, and maximum number of simultaneous users). Does the server have a specific application it runs or tasks for which it is responsible? If LUL is going to place electronic databases in a networked

Figure 1
The First Layer of the Topological Technology Map

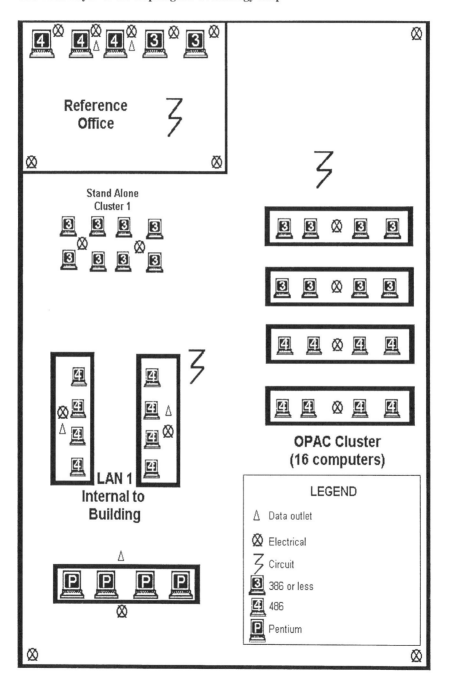

environment, the administration will have to know if the existing servers can handle the additional load or if a new server is needed. The more information included in the LUL topological technology map, the easier it will be to see where improvements are needed and where strengths already exist.

The data and electrical portion of the first layer will show exactly where the electrical outlets and data lines are found in the library, floor by floor. It will be useful to the LUL administration and the University Physical Plant to identify weaknesses in both electrical and data access which might impede progress toward the library's goals. The map can also illustrate how many electrical circuits the LUL library has in each public and department area. The number of circuits is important because, as more powerful equipment is brought on-line, the lack of sufficient circuits may lead to an increase in the possibilities of brown-outs. When this part of the first layer is completed, it will enhance and add value to information previously known about the computer equipment and outlets.[4]

The Second Layer of the Topological Technology Map: Format/Platform and Access

The second layer of the map illustrates the location of and the format/platform of the library's electronic resources. This layer should be quick to plot because whatever method for noting (symbols or colors), the map shows where the resources, such as the CD-ROM stand-alone cluster or the local area network (LAN), are located and if they have a serial connection or a campus backbone connection. While noting the format of the electronic products, the mapper should also note the platform (DOS, Windows 3.x, Windows 95, and so on) of the products, as knowing the platform of a resource helps to identify which resources can be easily moved into a Windows or Web-based network environment and which will need to be upgraded. For example, if LUL upgrades to Windows 95, DOS platform products will be able to continue to operate. However, if LUL upgrades to Windows NT, the DOS platform products will have to be upgraded also to function on a NT network, as Windows NT does not acknowledge the existence of DOS.

Once this information is gathered and mapped, the second layer is completed and can be laid upon the first to give a complete picture of the information technology structure of the library (see Figure 2). LUL administration and staff now have a visual picture of the task ahead of them as they carry out their technology upgrade plan.

Topological Technology Map of the Campus

The library's completed map provides a dense, multilayered picture of the library's information technology infrastructure. In addition the library's administration and Systems Office staff should also map the computer and data

Figure 2
The Second Layer of the Topological Technology Map

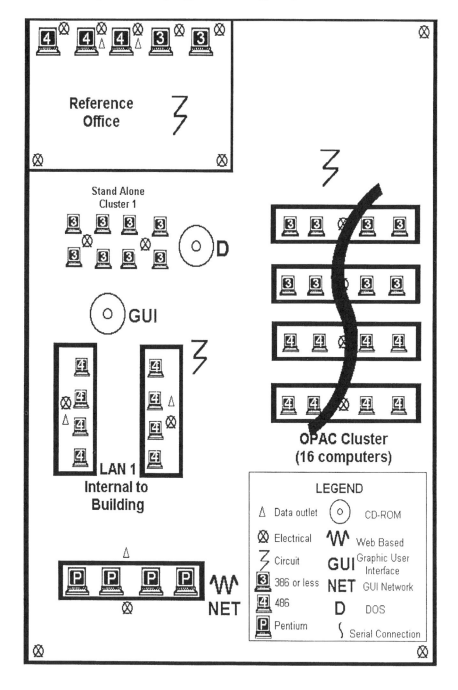

access on the entire campus. The bulk of many library budgets are spent on purchasing site licenses for remote access, but if the campus is not adequately connected, the campus community cannot take advantage of the information resources, thus wasting money and making promises that cannot be fulfilled with resources available; that is, with apologies, the library should not write a check the campus cannot cash.

For example, LUL has planned to move all of its electronic resources to a network for easy remote access by the faculty, staff, and students. If only 30 percent of the campus classroom buildings and none of the dormitories are wired, the higher subscription cost the library is paying for on-campus remote access is not realized as a good enough return. On the other hand, as greater numbers of Luddite students become enrolled in distance education courses, the Library's investment will likely pay off. How do LUL and other university libraries find this vital information? It may be as easy as calling the campus computing center and asking what percentage of the campus is wired. There may be a campus computing facilities committee which would share such information, a committee which, incidentally, needs a library representative. If the library is not involved in such a committee, inquiries should be made as to how the library can become involved.

As information is gathered concerning the total campus infrastructure, the library administration should ask the campus community how it uses the electronic resources provided by the library. Although this would seem to be a truism, and obvious, many libraries fail to gather information from the very people they claim to serve. In Chapter 7 of this book Darlene Weingand discusses the importance of surveying the library's patron population. The patron survey will illustrate who is using the library (this may help in future product selections), where they are using the library resources (in the library, in their offices or dormitories, and /or other remote access), and how aware the campus community is of electronic resources and services provided.

Aside from the telephone or mailed patron survey, technology provides more objective patron measures. Transactional logs track the usage of databases. Libraries should avail themselves of this information to ensure that they provide access to resources that their patrons use. If the survey and the logs show that the services and electronic resources the library staff provide access to are not being used, the staff must also be willing to discontinue electronic resources and try others.

PUTTING THE TOPOLOGICAL TECHNOLOGY MAP TO USE

With the basic information technology infrastructure charted, the library administration can now begin to respond to change quickly with in-depth knowledge of the library's computers, data lines and electrical outlet locations, and the format/platform and access method of the library's electronic resources.

At LUL, the administration and the staff can use the maps to realize their own technology upgrade plan. As a member of CONE, LUL wants to implement a new Web-based automation system which will require that all public workstations have backbone/Internet connections and computers loaded with a graphical user interface (GUI) operating system with a Web browser. If LUL administrators look at the map (Figure 1), they will notice that currently LUL has eighteen 386s, nineteen 486s, and four Pentiums on the first floor. To run the new automation system, the 386s and the 486s will have to be replaced. The four Pentiums may be upgradable. What type of computer should the LUL Systems Office buy? The maps will help the library to position itself to take advantage of new technology.

For both the public and the staff computers, the Systems Office should purchase a high-end processor, with double the RAM required by the operating system and a video card. Staff computer needs will be dependent upon the staff's task; for cataloging staff who will spend a majority of their time in front of the computer screen, the Systems Office staff should add a 17-inch monitor to the cataloging computers and increase the RAM so that catalogers can take advantage of multitasking in a graphical environment. For public services staff, a laptop computer in addition to a network computer on their desk would allow the staff to go to wired classrooms to teach or work at home, transferring information through the networked computer to the server.

One of the strengths of CONE and LUL's Web-based catalog is the inclusion of links from within the catalog to video and audio through the Internet. Patrons will have pertinent auditory or visual information in addition to traditional bibliographic information. To provide that for the patrons, the Systems Office should add a sound card to the public workstations. Because of the public location, headphones instead of speakers will allow the patron to hear.

Replacing all the computers at once would be expensive; however, phasing in necessary computers over several years may be desirable. LUL could also decide to try a computer alternative; for example, they could replace the computers in the public area with networked computers, which are cheaper, as all of their software resides on a server. LUL may not have considered all of these options had they not created a map to provide the hard cold reality during discussions.

In meetings to examine LUL's computer possibilities, the LUL administrators can use the map to assess the three servers (see Figure 1). The map shows that LUL has a dedicated server running the current automation system, one that runs the library's Internet gateway, and one server that runs the internal LAN. For LUL, the server for the automation system goes back to the CONE consortium after the conversion to the Web-based system and thus is not considered in any of the discussion. The LAN server is found incapable of running the new automation system, but the Systems Office staff may be able to use it to serve the CD-ROM products on the new network.

The LUL Internet gateway server may be the one to upgrade and use as the main server. It will run client and server software for the new automation system, and it will also serve the pages from the LUL's new digitization project for the library. The server already has the capacity to handle 250 simultaneous users, and with a staff of 140, including the staff in the branch library located in the School of Mines, the user level is adequate, but the LUL administration and Systems Office staff will have to decide if they need to plan for expanding beyond the 250 number as the server takes on the additional tasks of the new automation system and serving pages from the digital project. If the administration decides to buy a new server, the Systems Office staff and the administration should plan to buy a server with more computing power than they need currently.

The next step for LUL is to examine its map to determine the connectivity of the library (see Figure 1). Currently, LUL has only fourteen workstations with data connections, and it will need to connect the remaining 27 computers to the server. The LUL group, which hopefully has a copy of this book, may refer to Chapter 4, in which Clifton Dale Foster and Steven J. Bell discuss wireless technology, to see if this technology will offer any solutions for connectivity. For example, the LUL Systems Office could go wireless in the public area and move the backbone connections and the etherwaves to the staff areas, or vice versa.

While investigating the number of connections, the LUL Systems Office staff will need to examine the adequacy of the library's electrical outlets (see Figure 1). They may want to add outlets to lessen the dependence on power strips in the public area. The Systems Office staff and the physical plant staff may also want to add electrical circuits to ensure that the library will not lose power in its public areas as it adds more powerful equipment on to the existing circuits.

Even after LUL takes the plunge and purchases all of the new equipment and new operating systems, the administration will still need to rely on the map to make further decisions on products to purchase. The map shows a stand-alone cluster of DOS-based CD-ROM stations on the main floor (see Figure 2). The products on that cluster will have to be upgraded to run in a GUI environment. If they do not have a GUI version of, for example, the Tropical Bird Search database, the LUL staff will have to consider its options. They may choose a different vendor for the same database or they may drop the product. If the product is infrequently used, according to the patron survey and transactional log, perhaps the staff can cancel the product and try a different product in the same subject area, such as the Bird SearchPro database. In addition, the products on the existing network will need to be integrated into the new network configuration. The Systems Office staff will need to implement software that will track the number of simultaneous users for each product, rejecting requests for connection when the maximum number of simultaneous users is reached.

LUL should also consider purchasing Web-based electronic resources from the CONE consortium. Consortiums have been traditionally defined in geographic terms, such as within an x mile radius, statewide, or neighboring states.

They have organized themselves to take advantage of cooperative collection development and price breaks for electronic resources. CONE can offer consortium-wide access as part of the Web-based OPAC or as a separate grouping of databases. By working with the consortium, LUL can stretch its budget and increase the number of databases it can provide to its patrons.

Consortiums and vendors use several formulas when negotiating the cost of a subscription. The formula most often used by consortiums today is the group discount rates for access to electronic products. These agreements allow for cost to be spread out to all members based on an agreed-upon formula. One alternative formula allows each member to pay for one resource and the vendor provides access to the resource for the whole consortium. For example, LUL decides to purchase access to the Tropical Bird Search database from Zippy Vendors. As a part of the agreement, Zippy Vendors provides access to the database for all CONE members as long as another CONE subscribes to another database Zippy offers, such as the Wallabies of the Wild.

The new automation system may also offer LUL and CONE an opportunity to expand their electronic holdings. The vendor of the new system may offer its own grouping of databases that patrons may search without having to leave the familiar interface of the OPAC. The new system may also allow for CONE and LUL to use the Z39.5 standard to connect with other libraries or electronic databases. The maps should help to stimulate the discussion on which databases to subscribe to, whether to go with the consortium, and the access method.

CONCLUDING REMARKS

LUL's many decisions are a few examples of how knowledge of today's library can help to launch the library of tomorrow. LUL can become a very agile place (even with all those Luddites). After closely reviewing its topographical technology map and taking several steps, the map can help the library to envision its future. The topological technology map can help an agile library plot, play with, and plan for its technology resources, to identify all of its possible futures.

NOTES

1. To read more about planning for library building construction see Richard J. Bazillion and Connie Braun (1995), *Academic Libraries as High-Tech Gateways: A Guide to Design and Space Decisions* (Chicago: American Library Association). The first chapter includes many practical considerations that can be applied to building in old spaces.

2. Peter Drucker (1970), *Technology, Management, and Society* (New York: Harper & Row), p. 131. Erik Delfino wrote an article in the March/April 1995 issue of *Online* which examines the development of a spreadsheet/database tracking system. The floor plans for new buildings and renovations often show where computers will be located but rarely do they show the level of detail represented in this map.

3. The first layer of the map can be plotted on grid paper or created with a computer graphical software, such as Visio. The second layer is drawn on a transparency or rice paper, laid on top of the first map. You do not have to map a whole floor, smaller units such as the Reference Office area can be mapped separately if greater detail is needed.

4. In *University Library Building Planning* (Metuchen, N.J.: Scarecrow Press, 1990, p. 105), Heather M. Edwards includes an electricity checklist which includes circuits and connectors.

REFERENCE

Drucker, Peter. 1970. *Technology, Management, and Society*. New York: Harper & Row.

ANNOTATED BIBLIOGRAPHY

Bazillion, Richard J., and Connie Braun. 1995. *Academic Libraries as High-Tech Gateways: A Guide to Design and Space Decisions*. Chicago: American Library Association. A thought-provoking book that examines the many steps involved in building a new library that incorporates the new information technology and the role of libraries in the new information era.

Cline, Nancy M. 1994. "Local or Remote Access: Choices and Issues." In *Electronic Access to Information: A New Service Paradigm*. Proceedings from a Symposium held in Palo Alto, Calif., July 23–24, 1993. Research Libraries Group, pp. 17–24. The author challenges the reader to realize that electronic access changes how we evaluate research libraries. She also notes that remote and local access loses its meaning in an electronic world. Selection in the electronic world is a complicated decision-making process in which the final selection must "benefit our students, faculty and others we serve" (p. 17).

Eaton, Nancy L. 1994. "Computing Resources: Opportunities and Challenges in Institutional Cooperation." In Peggy Johnson and Bonnie MacEwan (eds.), *Collection Management and Development: Issues in An Electronic Era*. Proceedings of the Advanced Collection Management and Development Institute, March 26–28, 1993. Chicago: American Library Association, pp. 80–91. This chapter examines cooperative electronic collection development. The author notes three types of cooperative models: intralibrary, intracampus, and geographical. For the technologically agile library, cooperative models can help to stretch budgets by removing the hardware requirements of servers while meeting the research needs of its patrons.

Molholt, Pat. 1993. "Libraries as Bridges: Librarians as Builders." In F. W. Lancaster (ed.), *Libraries and the Future: Essays on the Library and the Twentieth Century*. New York: Haworth Press, pp. 17–28. The author examines the trends of technology and identifies issues such as the speed of obsolescence of technology, equipment budget shortfalls, and the upheaval of constant change. The rest of the chapter focuses on change as challenging opportunities for librarians.

Pitkin, Gary M. 1995. *Impact of Emerging Technologies on Reference Services and Bibliographic Instruction*. Westport, Conn.: Greenwood Press. The chapters by George Machovec, "Identifying Emerging Technologies" (pp. 1-23) and Delmus Williams, "People, Organization and Information Technology: Facing the Millennium'' (pp. 75–94) challenge the academic librarian to think in broader terms of technology. Machovec examines the trends of technology and its impact on the total library. He describes a library where the processes of collection development, acquisition, and delivery come together to provide the patron with a wealth of resources. Williams suggests that while technology integrates services for librarians who are comfortable with the status quo, technology might take them outside the library to work with the patron in his /her department or dormitory building.

The Technologically Agile Library

4

The Agile Technology Manager: Adapting New Technologies to Connect People with Information

Clifton Dale Foster and Steven J. Bell

INTRODUCTION

Libraries and information technology are so deeply integrated that it would be impossible to discuss the qualities of agile managers without a consideration of the role information technology plays in the development of successful library organizations. One challenge in providing guidance for managing information technology is in determining which technology to discuss. From automation systems to World Wide Web (WWW) resources, library managers must be familiar with a myriad of technologies and have the ability to effectively decide which to acquire, and to determine how they are best deployed. Even with a single technology, there may be a host of complex issues.

Consider the deployment of the on-line public access catalog (OPAC). In today's information environment, how is the OPAC best made available to the library's constituency? Generally, three interface options are available: Windows GUI (Graphical Users Interface), Web (GUI plus hypertext), and ASCII (character based). For library managers, selecting one interface over another is not a simple choice because of the complexity of the issues involved. For one, all have different levels of functionality. While the Windows client may offer the greatest functionality, it raises problems related to software distribution. The Web client may offer the most hospitable user interface with a balance of high functionality, but will isolate library users without access to the Web. The ASCII client, though offering low-level functionality, will be demanded by patrons who dislike graphical user interfaces, do not have Windows-capable computer equipment, or who value searching speed and command-style searching over the newer interfaces.

Despite the greater burden placed on library staff to support three different OPAC clients, the complexity of the technology may require the manager to offer all three interfaces. The agile manager needs to meet the demands of a diverse constituency and must be technologically sophisticated enough to develop and implement the appropriate solutions to resolve these challenges. This is but one example of the challenges library managers face in delivering information to their clientele. In this chapter we present a case study of sorts that examines how an agile manager can harness one technology, wireless data communications, to offer solutions to real information delivery problems. This will demonstrate how agile library organizations can integrate new technology to resolve the problems library managers confront in their effort to connect people and information, which, in essence, is what libraries are all about.

THE TECHNOLOGY DILEMMA: TWO CASES

Case One: The Bibliographic Instructor's Dilemma

Every fall, thousands of librarians at academic institutions prepare for a new onslaught of students. Accompanying the crush of students is an array of library-organized instruction programs designed to introduce students to library resources, and teach them how to properly use those resources. Things are no different at Madison Central College, a small, four-year liberal arts institution. Despite its small staff, Marilyn Peterson takes her responsibilities as the Electronic Instruction Librarian seriously. Though the school is small, the library is technologically sophisticated. Within the library, Marilyn has an exceptional set of resources for bibliographic instruction.

Outside the library, this college is technologically challenged. This became quite apparent to Marilyn when Professor Keller of the Political Science Department called. Keller asked Marilyn to develop a 45-minute instructional session that could be delivered in the classroom, designed to teach students the basics of using on-line data banks. Marilyn was quick to agree, and suggested a live demonstration to show students different data banks and practical search examples. The day before the presentation, Marilyn realized she had not made a previous presentation in the building where Keller's classroom was located. Though she planned to use her own notebook computer and liquid crystal display (LCD) panel, Marilyn decided to call the campus classroom support office to verify whether the room had an Ethernet connection or modem jack.

The staff member at classroom support informed her that Keller's classroom had neither. This particular building was yet to undergo a wiring renovation. This news was distressing, for it meant she had no means to connect to the campus network, and therefore, no way to present a live on-line demonstration.

Marilyn feared her on-line instruction would lack the sizzle that engaged students. Though disappointed, she decided to use some downloaded searches as examples. She wished there was another option for getting on-line.

Case Two: Networking on a Budget

John Hiller is the library director at Normal-Everyday University. Mr. Hiller considers himself quite fortunate. Despite difficult budgetary circumstances at the university, he managed to convince the provost of the importance of building a new library addition. Hiller envisions creating a dynamic electronic-research center as the core of the new facility. Unfortunately, funding for the project covered little beyond actual construction costs. His limited equipment budget will provide for the purchase of the necessary computer equipment, but the prospects of additional funding in the future seem unlikely.

Hiller and his staff are in the process of planning the physical layout of the new wing to accommodate banks of networked computer terminals. He knows from experience that flexibility is a major advantage, allowing for versatile desk and shelving arrangements. He also knows that running computer network cabling is expensive, and moving computer terminals to non-cabled areas of the building is problematic. Given the unlikelihood of additional library funding for computer equipment in the near future, Hiller knows he must make the right decision the first time. He labors over just where he should locate computer terminals and associated network cable connections. The ideal solution would allow him to cost-effectively move terminals as the space utilization needs of his library change.

TECHNOLOGY AS A TOOL FOR THE AGILE MANAGER

Creating the agile library is the responsibility of library managers. We differentiate the manager from the administrator. The latter performs routine, assigned job functions designed to maintain organizational operation, while the former assumes responsibility for the futurity of the organization through creative leadership and risk taking. Agile managers are adept at using available tools to resolve challenges and reshape their libraries. Technology may be viewed as a tool that is a means for accomplishing some end. In each of the scenarios presented above, the appropriate management of technology offered a solution. What is the problem? As we see it, libraries must use technology to develop better ways, for an increasingly mobile population, to connect people with the information they seek.

From our perspective, the agile library manager is a technology manager. What do technology managers do? The core of that role is described as follows by Edward Roberts, Professor of Management at Massachusetts Institute of Technology (Gaynor 1996, 1.3):

- Integrate technology in the organization's strategic objectives;
- Take a proactive stance in introducing new technologies into the organization's work processes;
- Increase the productivity and performance of staff members;
- Understand and work with professionals from other disciplines in managing projects;
- Analyze available resources and effectively determine where technology best serves the organization's infrastructure.

Technology management is a set of skills that agile managers use to harness resources and convert them into viable products and services. In a manufacturing enterprise, technology management results in innovative product development processes that are both more efficient and less costly. In libraries, technology management takes available technology and turns it into tools agile managers use to improve existing services and deliver new ones. What about the librarians in the two case studies? What technology could alleviate their problems? How might these library organizations harness new technology to better connect people to information?

Wireless data communication is the technology offered as the most viable solution. Thanks to WWW advancements, librarians are increasingly able to use the Internet as the primary conduit for delivering information to library constituents. We can provide access to more information more seamlessly than ever imagined. Though available on a fairly wide basis for at least five years, libraries have largely ignored the possibilities of integrating cellular and other wireless communication technologies with other technological tools.

The advent of cellular and other wireless technologies has produced one of the most significant changes in our society, primarily in business at first, but increasingly at the personal level. We are a mobile society. More time is spent between places, traveling by auto or plane. We communicate over longer distances, and now have the capacity to teach someone on the other side of the globe as easily as someone in a classroom on campus. The librarians in our cases were fictional, but their unenviable situations were not. Despite our mastery of many information technologies, the overwhelming majority of libraries and information centers are primitive in their knowledge and use of wireless communications technology.

As the age of Personal Communications Services (PCS) dawns, it is not unrealistic to picture a society where each person has their own individual phone or communicator. They will have the capability to communicate with other people and electronic devices from anywhere at any time. If libraries cannot meet the challenges today of making "anytime, anywhere" information accessibility possible on their own campuses, it does not bode well for our success in adapting to the wireless communication environment of the future. To maintain their agility, it will be critically important for library organizations to adapt to a rapidly changing wireless society.

A WIRELESS FUTURE: UNPLUGGING OUR LIBRARIES

Recent developments in the evolution of wireless data communication offer great potential for broadening access to library services in ways never before conceived. In fact, wireless network connectivity may be the next logical step in the evolution of library information systems.

Of utmost importance for technology managers is the versatility that wireless data networks can provide. Banks of public access computer terminals, once tethered to expensive network cabling, can be easily moved and rearranged as the changing space utilization needs of the library change. Another advantage offered by wireless networks is the ability to provide computer network access in buildings not suitable for wired networks. In situations where concrete walls or historic structures are involved, wireless communication technologies provide the best solution to network connectivity.

One of the most attractive aspects of wireless connectivity is the ability to break down the physical restraints of buildings or land-line telephones. Wireless connections provide a means for researchers to access on-line computer data when involved in field research many miles from the nearest library. For campus-wide information systems, wireless networks can supplement, or even replace, wire-based connectivity. The possibility of using packet radio, spread-spectrum, or microwave technology for connecting desktop/portable computers to university computer networks offers greater flexibility and certain cost savings. By using campus-wide wireless networks, college and university administrators could save millions of dollars they would otherwise spend on wiring buildings and rooms. Indeed, the mobility offered by wireless networks may be better than traditional wired versions at meeting the computing needs and habits of students and faculty.

Campus-wide wireless connectivity provides the ability for librarians to offer live, on-line bibliographic instruction sessions in more settings without regard for installed computer network wiring. The availability of a wireless network connecting campus buildings to the library's on-line catalog and the Internet would eliminate the dilemma of Marilyn Peterson, our fictional librarian. In the same way, wireless access to electronic library resources would have made John Hiller's difficult decision on locating networked workstations less problematic. The deployment of wireless networks not only allows increased access to library resources, but can provide greater flexibility in computer network management as well.

The phrase ''wireless data communications'' has become a catch-all for a variety of communication technologies which facilitate the transfer of information between electronic devices, without the use of telephone lines or network computer cabling. When looking at the wireless landscape, the technology manager is faced with numerous choices, each with its own benefits and shortcomings. For library applications, the basic types of wireless data transfer technologies currently available are cellular, packet-radio, wireless local area networks (LANs), and satellite data communications.

Perhaps the most familiar form of two-way wireless communication technology is analog cellular communication. In this system, transmission of data is much like cellular voice transmission in that it uses the same analog radio signals routed through circuit-switched networks. In the simplest configuration, a user can plug a desktop or laptop computer equipped with an analog modem into a cellular phone using a cellular data interface. Several PC Card modems currently available have the cellular data interface integrated into the modem.

Analog cellular data transmission has proven quite satisfactory for many library applications. It is certainly one of the least expensive wireless options in terms of equipment expenditures. In a direct comparison test of wired versus wireless connectivity for on-line searching, no noticeable quality differences in data transmission were detected (Bell and Halperin 1995). However, analog cellular connection charges can become quite expensive with cellular air-time fees ranging from $.18 to $.50 per minute. Also, since analog cellular systems are designed primarily for voice, they tend to be slow at carrying data. Speeds of up to only 9,600 bits per second are possible with any degree of reliability. For high-speed data-intensive operations other wireless alternatives should be explored.

Digital cellular technologies were developed, in part, to overcome some of the shortcomings of analog signals in delivering data. Three major types of digital cellular transmission technology are available for use in the United States—Time Division Multiple Access Code (TDMA), Code Division Multiple Access (CDMA), and Cellular Digital Packet Data (CDPD). Additionally, the Global System for Mobiles (GSM) is currently the digital standard in Europe and over 40 other countries. By translating analog signals into digital format, these digital cellular technologies provide faster transmission speeds and greater reliability of data. TDMA multiplexes several data bit streams over the same frequency channel using controlled time slots. CDMA assigns a unique code to each data bit stream and allows the data to travel over multiple frequency channels. CDPD uses idle air time on analog voice channels to transmit packets of digitally encoded data over multiple frequencies. CDPD has the advantage of offering built-in Transmission Control Protocol/Internet Protocol (TCP/IP) commonly used over the wired Internet network. GSM is a TDMA-based standard which is gaining attention in the United States for possible deployment in PCS systems. The availability of digital cellular technologies varies greatly from locality to locality. Technology managers should check with cellular service providers to identify the availability of digital cellular services in their area.

Packet radio is a digital mode of communication used extensively by amateur radio enthusiasts. In a packet-radio data transmission system, the computer modem is replaced by a terminal node controller (TNC). The telephone is replaced by a radio transceiver, and the phone network is replaced by radio waves. Packet radio takes data sent from the computer and sends it via radio to another radio station similarly equipped.

For libraries, the major advantages in packet-radio networks are that transmission costs are minimal (once initial operating equipment is purchased), TCP/IP is available as a transmission protocol, and no Federal Communications Commission (FCC) licenses are required to operate within assigned frequencies. The drawbacks are that coverage is limited to line-of-sight and, at this time, library computer applications taking advantage of packet-radio technology are limited.

Wireless local area networks (LANs) do the same thing as conventional computer LANs, only without the need to lay costly phone lines or coaxial cables throughout a building or campus. Three types of wireless LANs are available—infrared, microwave, and spread-spectrum.

Infrared data transmission systems use intense light beams to transmit data faster than many other wireless LAN technologies. Infrared devices are less expensive than other wireless LAN devices, but not as economical as standard network cards. The drawbacks of infrared systems are that they are limited to line-of-sight transmission, sending and receiving units must be closely aligned, and the data path must be kept unobstructed by walls or furniture.

Microwave signals allow high-speed data transfer rates and have the advantage of penetrating walls. They can also support applications requiring full-motion video transmission and point-to-multipoint broadcasting. Microwave-based LANs have the same drawbacks as infrared systems in that transmission is limited to distances up to fifteen miles, sending and receiving units must be closely aligned, and the data path must be unobstructed. Microwave systems have been used with success in deploying wide-area networks (WANs) for multi-campus educational institutions. With the current state of microwave technology, these systems can offer substantial cost savings over leased lines and fiber optic connections.

A spread-spectrum system is one in which the transmitted signal is spread over a wide frequency band—much wider, in fact, than the minimum bandwidth required to transmit the data being sent. Some systems use "frequency hopping" to jump around the assigned array of channels. Other systems use a faster direct-sequence spread-spectrum (DSSS) technique. AT&T's WaveLAN, Proxim's RangeLAN2, and RadioLAN's RadioLAN/10 are examples of spread-spectrum systems currently available for IBM/PC compatible systems. Digital Ocean provides a similar system for the Apple Newton. Spread-spectrum signals can penetrate walls and can reach transmission speeds of up to 10 Mbps and a range of up to 1,200 feet.

The lack of standards, high prices, and perceived low transmission speeds have been the main issues suppressing wireless LAN development. However, wireless LANs will soon become more economical and more reliable for libraries due to two recent events—FCC approval of the National Information

Infrastructure (NII) band of frequencies for high-capacity, unlicensed wireless data use and the soon-to-be-released IEEE 802.11 wireless LAN standard. The NII band provides free unlicensed operation of wireless devices in the 5 GHz frequency range, thereby making wireless connectivity a cost-effective alternative for schools and libraries. The new IEEE 802.11 standard will allow similar wireless LAN technologies to interoperate; it will also enable wireless LANs to work with existing wired LAN technologies such as Ethernet and token ring.

Satellite data transmission, once only within the financial reach of large universities, entertainment corporations, and government agencies, may soon "come down to earth." Teledesic Corp., a joint venture of Microsoft's Bill Gates, and Craig McCaw of McCaw Cellular, plans to have a fleet of several hundred orbiting satellites by the year 2002 which will allow two-way Internet connectivity via satellite disk. Hughes Network Systems already have something similar in place with its DirecPC system. This system uses a 24-inch KU-band satellite dish to receive Internet data from a satellite and send it directly to PCs equipped with the necessary expansion card. Data from PCs to the Internet still must be sent through modems connected to normal phone lines or integrated services digital network (ISDN) lines. Similarly, Sky Station International, Inc., has recently received FCC approval to implement a stratospheric Internet communications network using helium-filled blimps positioned some thirteen miles above the earth. Such "Internet-in-the-sky" approaches may offer libraries and information seekers greater access options and reduced costs to Internet-based information services.

Because of the hybrid nature of wireless data communications as applied in libraries, analysis of these technologies must necessarily be integrated into an evaluation of personal computer technologies, local wireless availability, and national telecommunication policies. The agile manager will need to survey the entire technological landscape in order to make decisions based on all available options. Given the three- to five-year useful life span of most personal computer equipment and the budget limitations of many libraries, determining the appropriate technology for computer networking requires real planning savvy.

MAKING TECHNOLOGY DECISIONS: EVALUATING COMPARABLE TECHNOLOGIES

Library managers are decision makers. Like everything else in the changing library environment, decision making isn't what it used to be. There is still a daily melange of routine decisions that an experienced administrator will make in split seconds, based on experience and intuition; but in certain areas, and technology is one of them, making good decisions is tough work. Why? In rapidly changing environments there is far greater uncertainty. When you can't accurately predict where things are headed, it is difficult to make a decision today that puts the library on the path to tomorrow.

In the past, it was fairly safe to make decisions based on forecasting probability. Ten years ago the typical academic institution's demographic was primarily 18- to 22-year-olds who resided on campus and completed degrees in four years. Print and electronic media were fairly stable. The library could make technology acquisitions with safe assurances that their future user groups would continue to have the same needs as in the past, and that the same CDs, OPACs, and computer workstations would deliver the goods. What's different is the growing number of high-impact changes that have no probability.

What library manager made technology acquisitions or planned for library service delivery based on the advent of the World Wide Web? None, because no one determined the probability it would be created or the impact it would have as the primary conduit for electronic information. Agile managers, when making decisions, can no longer depend on probability. In times of great change, they need to ask, ''What has already happened that will create the future?'' That is what our institutions are doing in planning the colleges and universities of the future. Environmental scanning and demographic, societal, and technology trend analysis are all utilized to determine what an academic institution will need to survive and prosper 10 or 20 years from now (Drucker 1995, 40).

While many libraries do not presently make use of wireless technology to provide access to electronic information, based on what we know is already happening, our students will be much more in tune with wireless technology in the near future. The proliferation of cellular phones, the decreasing costs of cellular air time, the widespread availability of PCS, and the development of satellite networks for global wireless service indicate that people will expect libraries to serve as the gateway to electronic information and to provide that information anywhere at any time. Therefore, a critical information technology decision for positioning the future library is how to deliver information wirelessly. With competing technologies to choose from, how does one decide wisely?

Consider the multiple wireless technologies we have introduced. Is cellular a better choice than packet-radio, or will a wireless local area network better serve the library's needs? Which of today's technologies will be here tomorrow, or is most adaptable to technological change? How does one decide? Based on past research in comparing competing wireless technologies, as well as evaluating the comparable effectiveness of wired and wireless on-line connectivity, we recommend how the agile manager can proceed in making comparative technology decisions.

Start by thoroughly understanding where your institution is positioned with respect to this technology. What is the telecommunications office doing with wireless technology? Is the classroom support office integrating wireless technology into educational programs? Becoming knowledgeable about the institutional application of any technology has a critical function. It will identify what opportunities for collaboration exist or determine if the library will need to take initiative for pioneering a new technology within the organization. If the organization has already established cellular as the wireless technology to acquire, the library can achieve more support for plans to integrate wireless services. Opting for a competing technology may still be the library's choice, and if the agile library manager demands it, it may be possible. Expect more difficulty in obtaining funding from the organization and support from the organizational infrastructure. The importance of collaboration in technology acquisitions cannot be underestimated.

Next, be equally knowledgeable about the state-of-the-art in wireless technologies—not only on a national level, but on a local level as well. While it is important to know what the different technological offerings are within the scope of an industry, not all of those options may be available on a local level. One's particular geographic placement may be a deciding factor. Even the location of a building may be a factor. Some wireless technologies do not work well in dense urban locations with many high-rise buildings or are not well-suited for certain facilities, such as windowless or basement rooms. Deciding among competing wireless technologies may require on-site visits by vendors to demonstrate the systems. This will establish if the transmission quality is satisfactory, whether accessibility and speed are acceptable, and what the projected costs are for the service.

Finally, take time to discuss the integration of this new technology with two important groups: staff and users. Collaboration with external offices is important, but pales in comparison to the value of staff buy-in on new technology acquisitions. Successful implementation is unlikely without support from the front line of the organization. Consider user support issues. Satisfaction with the new technology depends on staff ability to train new users, assist them in adapting to the new system, and provide ongoing support. If the library staff finds the new technology confusing or difficult to operate, it is unlikely that they will invest their time to master the technology. The agile manager knows the value of staff input and recognizes the stress induced by technological change. Therefore, managing in times of technological change demands responsiveness to staff needs.

While user input is valued, the agile manager is careful not to let constituents dictate the library's technological decisions. If their role as shareholders in the decision process is not made clear, user input can go awry. Their attitudes and concerns about new technology need to be solicited, but users should be well informed that the final decision power rests with the library administration. Deciding which of several competing technologies to choose from can be aided when we know how our users will take advantage of it, what their current levels of use and sophistication are, and how the existing service fails to satisfy their needs and specific changes that can rectify that situation.

Good technology decisions, such as choosing the best wireless alternative from among an array of rapidly changing options, require some basic knowledge:

• know the institution
• know the technology
• know the staff
• know the users

This information will help the agile manager make decisions that lead to successful outcomes during times of great change.

BEYOND THE WALLS: LIBRARY APPLICATIONS OF WIRELESS TECHNOLOGY

Several pilot projects have demonstrated both the promises and pitfalls of wireless technologies in academic and library environments. Over 15 years ago, a group of researchers at the University of California experimented with a packet-radio network for linking library computers in the San Francisco area (Brownrigg et al. 1984). Some eight years ago, public librarians demonstrated the possibilities of using cellular data transmission to connect bookmobiles with centralized on-line library catalogs (Logsdon 1990). More recently, the University of South Alabama Library demonstrated the feasibility of using hand-held personal digital assistants (PDAs) equipped with cellular modems in a library environment (Foster 1995). For the most part, large-scale projects designed to fully implement wireless data communications in libraries can be characterized by jump starts and sudden stops. In retrospect, these projects serve to identify both technological and financial barriers to success. Two notable exceptions are currently in the process of reevaluating the promise of wireless technologies in academic settings.

The Wireless Andrew project began in the fall of 1994 at Carnegie Mellon University. This project seeks to make the full functionality and services of Carnegie Mellon's on-campus wired computing system (known as Andrew) available by wireless means (Hills and Johnson 1996). Services include e-mail, access to stored audio and imaging data, file transfers, access to the library and other databases, and full Internet services.

This project is developing a communications infrastructure based on two separate but interconnected wireless networks. Using AT&T's WaveLAN wireless LAN technology, a high-speed (2 Mbps) wireless data network is used to provide coverage over a large portion of the campus. Outside the wireless LAN service area, a lower-speed (19.2 Kbps) CDPD service is being developed to provide coverage of parts of the Pittsburgh metropolitan area. Users access the networks using laptop computers equipped with wireless LAN interface cards and on-board CDPD modems. Software to allow seamless movement between the wireless LAN and CDPD networks is being developed.

A related project began in 1995 at the University of California at Santa Cruz

(DeLoughry 1995). A campus-wide wireless network was developed by Metricom Inc. using their proprietary Ricochet technology. The nine-month pilot project, which involved fifteen students on the 2,000-acre campus, is among the most comprehensive attempts at exploring how the fledgling technology could be used in higher education.

The Ricochet network employed spread-spectrum packet radios installed geographically in a mesh topology. Metricom mounted 50 radio transceivers on the tops of street lights and buildings. Students were provided with special wireless modems that connected to the network.

The system proved reliable during the university's trial period. Students were able to connect to the campus network and to the Internet from virtually anywhere on campus. The speed of the connection, an important factor for the transfer of large graphical image files, was at least as good as what was available to dormitory residents who must use the telephone to dial into the campus network. Transmission speeds ranged from 14.4 Kbps to 34 Kbps, depending on network traffic. Computers wired directly to the campus Ethernet network were much faster, sometimes reaching speeds of 10 Mbps. Users of the wireless network also had full Internet connections, which meant that they could look at World Wide Web pages as well as review their electronic mail. Metricom currently has the Ricochet wireless network installed on nine other university campuses across the country.

These pilot projects demonstrate how real managers are using wireless connectivity on university campuses to solve real problems. These projects serve as examples of what can be done given the current state of wireless technology. The increasing installed base of CDPD cellular systems and spread-spectrum based wireless LANs should reduce communication costs associated with these technologies and make them more economically attractive for educational institutions. Certainly more research and development is needed, and is indeed anticipated given the recent approval of the NII band and a perceived expanding commercial market for wireless products. These recent technological and regulatory developments favor increased development of wireless devices for school and library use.

SUMMARY/CONCLUSION

In an age of catch-phrase proliferation, we find ourselves adding one more to the heap. As advocates of wireless data communications, we speak often of a coming age of "anytime, anywhere communication." Clearly, the technology for such an environment is evolving, but there is still much progress required. As our discussion of these technologies indicates, some, such as packet-radio systems are well developed but far from ubiquitous, while others, such as satellite networks, are not far removed from the drawing board.

How does "anytime, anywhere communication" relate to the skills and competencies required of agile library managers? Our discussion of wireless data communication illustrates how technology applications may solve practical problems that constrain our ability to meet library users' needs. There are any number of evolving and existing technologies that might fit into a discussion of the ways in which a new system or product can improve library operations. The point we want to stress is that agile library organizations will succeed in an environment of change through an awareness of new technologies, an openness to exploring them, and a willingness to adapt them to existing services.

In order for that to happen, the agile library manager needs to be hospitable to new possibilities. Most wireless data communication technologies are still evolving. Such is the state of flux in the wireless marketplace, that making predictions related to the what, when, where, and how much of these services is beyond our grasp. We do know they hold great promise for improving the librarian's ability to eliminate barriers between people and the information they seek. Agile library managers will recognize that evolving technologies like wireless, hold vast potential to make our library organizations simpler to use in a changing environment that we expect to grow ever more complex.

FOR MORE INFORMATION

Additional information on wireless data communication in libraries can be found on the Wireless Libraries Homepage (http://www.duc.auburn.edu/~fostecd/docs/wireless.html) maintained at Auburn University Library. This site contains an interactive bibliography of printed publications and Internet resources relevant to wireless library applications.

For a broader view of wireless research and wireless products, not all focusing necessarily on libraries or educational applications, consult the University of Washington's World Wide Web Virtual Library: Mobile and Wireless Computing Homepage (http://snapple.cs.washington.edu:600/mobile/mobile_www.html).

REFERENCES

Bell, Steven J., and Michael Halperin. 1995. ''Online Unplugged: Testing the Reliability of Cellular Online Searching.'' *Online* 19 (September/October): 15–24.

Brownrigg, Edwin B., Clifford A. Lynch, and Rebecca L. Pepper. 1984. ''Packet Radio for Library Automation.'' *Information Technology and Libraries* 3 (September): 229–244.

DeLoughry, Thomas J. 1995. ''No Wires: An Alternative to Cabled Computing Passes a Test at Santa Cruz.'' *The Chronicle of Higher Education* (July 7): A15–A16.

Drucker, Peter F. 1995. *Managing in a Time of Great Change.* New York: Truman Talley.

Foster, Clifton Dale. 1995. ''PDA's and the Library Without a Roof.'' *Journal of Computing in Higher Education* 7 (Fall): 85–93.

Gaynor, Gerard H. 1996. ''Management of Technology: Description, Scope and Impli-

cations." In Gerard H. Gaynor (ed.), *Handbook of Technology Management* (pp. 1.3–1.31). New York: McGraw-Hill.
Hills, Alex, and David B. Johnson. 1996. "A Wireless Data Network Infrastructure at Carnegie Mellon University." *IEEE Personal Communications* 3 (February): 56–63.
Logsdon, Lori. 1990. "Bookmobile Online Circulation Via Cellular Telephone." *Computers in Libraries* 10 (April). 17–18.

ANNOTATED BIBLIOGRAPHY

The books and articles cited below are provided to give the reader a selective overview of management issues and practical applications of wireless data communications in libraries. It is by no means comprehensive.

Bell, Steven J. 1991. "Online without the Line: Cellular Technology for Searching on the Go." *Online* 15 (September): 15–25. The first of three articles by the author which address the application of online database searching using wireless (cellular) connectivity. Describes computer system configurations necessary for cellular data communications and evaluates the prospects of integrating cellular connectivity in library environments. Other articles that address this issue are Steven J. Bell, (1994), "How Much Longer Before It All Works: What Online Searchers Should Know About Wireless Data Communications," *Online* 18 (January): 45–52; Steven J. Bell and Michael Halperin (1995), "Online Unplugged: Testing the Reliability of Cellular Online Searching," *Online* 19 (September/October): 15–24.
Brownrigg, Edwin B., Clifford A. Lynch, and Rebecca L. Pepper. 1984. "Packet Radio for Library Automation." *Information Technology and Libraries* 3 (September): 229–244. Pioneering research and the first publication to thoroughly examine the application of wireless data communications in library environments. Describes research performed as part of the California State Library Packet Radio Project. The authors continued their exploration of this technology in Clifford A. Lynch and Edwin B. Brownrigg (1986), "Progress in Wide-Area Packet Radio," in Julie M. Hurd (ed.), *Proceedings of the 49th ASIS Annual Meeting* (Medford, N.J.: Published for the American Society for Information Science by Learned Information, Inc.) and in Edwin B. Brownrigg (1992), "Continuing Development of California State Packet Radio Project," *Proceedings of the ASIS Mid-Year Meeting* (Medford, N.J.: American Society for Information Science).
Cleveland, Gary. 1993. *Packet Radio: Applications for Libraries in Developing Countries. UDT Series on Data Communications Technologies and Standards for Libraries, Report No. 5*. Ottawa, Canada: International Federation of Library Associations and Institutions, International Office for UDT. Available at http://www.nlc-bnc.ca/ifla/VI/5/reports/rep5/rep5.htm. A thorough and in-depth study of packet radio deployment in developing nations where land-based communications are unreliable or absent. Examines the potential for this technology to increase access to library services and enhance resource sharing. Also evaluates the impediments to achieving these goals.
Cummings, Karen. 1995. "Wireless Technology Brings the State Library of Iowa On-

line.'' *Computers in Libraries* 15 (November-December): 26–27. Describes the experience of automating an aging building with thick walls and faulty wiring. A wireless local area network was developed to connect computers in the building with the library's central computer.

Foster, Clifton Dale. 1995. ''PDA's and the Library Without a Roof.'' *Journal of Computing in Higher Education* 7 (Fall): 85–93. Description of a pilot project to test the feasibility of connecting hand-held Personal Digital Assistants (PDAs) to library on-line catalogs using wireless (cellular) connectivity.

———. 1997. ''A Wireless Future: College and University Libraries Unplugged.'' *Proceedings of the 1996 CAUSE Annual Conference: Broadening Our Horizons—Information, Services, Technology*, Elizabeth Harris (ed.) (Boulder, Colo.: CAUSE), pp. 5-8-1–5-8-10. Available at http://www.cause.org/information-resources/ir-library/abstracts/cnc9640.html. Outlines the basic types of wireless data technologies currently available (cellular, packet-data, wireless LANS, and so on) and discusses the latest prototype projects to apply wireless technologies in educational and library settings. The technical feasibility of accessing library on-line public access catalogs, commercial on-line databases, and the Internet using wireless technologies are evaluated, along with the economic feasibility of wireless data communications.

Hills, Alex, and David B. Johnson. 1996. ''A Wireless Data Network Infrastructure at Carnegie Mellon University.'' *IEEE Personal Communications* 3 (February): 56–63. Describes the infrastructure of the Wireless Andrew Project and the characteristics of the two types of wireless networks (CDPD and wireless LANs) used. Very good technical overview for developing a campus-wide wireless network.

Logsdon, Lori. 1990. ''Bookmobile Online Circulation Via Cellular Telephone.'' *Computers in Libraries* 10 (April): 17–18. Logsdon provides one of the earliest evaluations of analog cellular telephone applications for public library use. For related experiences, see Catherine Suyak Alloway (1992), ''On the Road with Online: The Online Bookmobile,'' *Wilson Library Bulletin* 66 (May): 43–45; Mary Lou Pratt (1992), ''A Bookmobile Driver's Story,'' *Wilson Library Bulletin* 66 (May): 46–47.

Pearce, Frank H. P. 1993. ''Wireless Communications—Come in Dick Tracy!'' *Managing Information Technology as a Catalyst of Change*. Proceedings of the CAUSE Annual Conference (San Diego, Calif., December 7–10, 1993) (Boulder, Colo.: CAUSE), pp. 369–378. An overview of wireless technology as it relates to campus-wide networks. Discusses types of wireless communications technologies and the issues related to the use of wireless in an academic setting. Written from the perspective of a computing center manager.

Storm, David. 1995. ''A Sprawling Library with Concrete Walls Looks for Better LAN Technology.''*InfoWorld* 17 (March 20): 68. The first in a three-part series describing the experience of Johns Hopkins University's Welch Medical Library in connecting a concrete building to the library's central computer. See also David Storm (1996), ''Friday the 13th: A Horrific Day for Testing Wireless Network Solutions,'' *InfoWorld* 17 (March 27): 80; David Storm (1996), ''Wireless Links Prove Worse Than a Card Catalog for Giving a Reliable Connection,'' *InfoWorld* 17 (April 3): 60.

5

Outcome Measures for the Emerging Virtual Library

Thomas A. Peters

Virtual libraries appear to be emerging around every corner in cyberspace. The notion of a virtual library may be the controlling image for the new information era (Saunders and Mitchell 1996, 2). Although the nature, scope, usability, and usefulness of virtual libraries are being discussed in the literature and at conferences, all virtual libraries seem to offer organized, full-text (sometimes full-image) collections of computerized documents, along with nascent virtual public services. The heated debate about whether these emerging virtual libraries (EVLs) will overtake or overshadow paper-based, emerged real libraries (PERLs) is outside the scope of this chapter. Regardless of their status in relation to PERLs, EVLs will need to be evaluated. Eventually library managers will want and need to know how well EVLs are performing. This chapter contains an examination of possible ways to measure the performance, outputs, and outcomes of library services in a computerized, networked, virtual environment. The focus is on outcome measures for public services in emerging virtual libraries. Because this field is new, attention to fundamental issues appears to be necessary. While the emerging virtual library requires sophisticated and innovative thinking about both organizations and operations (Powell 1994), it also forces us to rethink some timeless themes: outcome measures, public services, and the aspects of libraries that transcend environmental factors. User-centered outcome measures will become a crucial way to assess the value of digital libraries.

WHAT IS AN EMERGING VIRTUAL LIBRARY (EVL)?

Traditional libraries are weighty edifices, bound in a situated place, filled with material objects (including humans) that store and convey information. The idea of a virtual library beckons us to both appreciate and rethink the massiveness and boundedness of libraries. Virtual libraries, if they emerge at all, will reside in some space called cyberspace. Our human sense of the nature of cyberspace continues to emerge. In order to realize a virtual library that conveys the depth, diversity, and richness we have come to expect from real libraries, we will need to develop a receptivity to a feeling of space that is not dependent on geographic space. Collectively we are old dogs, and it will be difficult to teach ourselves this new trick. To perform it with our accepted notion of a library, which relies on geographic space (for example, the academic library as the heart of the campus, or the public library as a fixture on the town square), will be a tall order. Libraries and their contents have been manageable (harkening back to the Latin root *manus*—the hand) for so long that it is difficult to imagine the diffusion and acceptance of a virtual library across a broad population of users.

It appears to be possible to develop a sense of space, especially in virtual environments, without having a sense of place as a prerequisite. We do not really know yet what sort of sense of information space will emerge after we get over the real space constraints that circumscribe real libraries. Unfortunately, the metaphor of real library space is being carried over to emerging virtual library environments, presumably because it facilitates the users' transition to a virtual information environment. The residual effects of the easy transition may include long-term stunted and pinched mental models of what a virtual information space could be.

The emerging virtual library can be difficult to define, or even recognize when encountered. Some critics have suggested that the concept has little if any identifiable meaning. For example, Crawford and Gorman (1995, 5) assert that the notion of a virtual library is an unchallenged confusion. They proceed (1995, 128) to suggest that the push for virtual libraries is a bizarre aspect of a new elitism. The term "virtual library" gained popularity in 1990 as reports about the formation of the Coalition for Networked Information (CNI) emphasized the goal of making a virtual library available to scholars, providing access to all information available electronically (Saunders and Mitchell 1996, 2–3).

Provisional definitions of virtual libraries abound. Powell (1994) sees at least three potential definitions of a virtual library. First, a virtual library could contain little or no physical collection of books, serials, reading space, or staff, yet electronically disseminate selective information directly to distributed library customers. Second, a virtual library could be a more traditional library that has converted significant portions of its information delivery channels into electronic format, so that many or most of its patrons do not need to physically visit the library in order to obtain information. Third, a virtual library could operate as a nexus of selected information management activities within an organization.

Some of the information management activities could be centralized, but most would happen through the efforts of decentralized staff, resources, systems, and even outside suppliers. Early in the development of the concept, Saunders (1996, 62) defined a virtual library as a computerized, networked computer system through which a user can connect transparently to remote libraries and databases using the local library's on-line catalog or a university or network computer as a gateway. Gapen (1993, 1) provides perhaps the longest definition of a virtual library:

The virtual library has been defined as the concept of remote access to the contents and services of libraries and other information resources, combining an on-site collection of current and heavily used materials in both print and electronic form, with an electronic network which provides access to, and delivery from, external worldwide library and commercial information and knowledge sources. In essence the user is provided the effect of a library which is a synergy created by bringing together technologically the resources of many, many libraries and information services.

The virtual library is a meta-library, combining and virtually comprehending all formats, collections, and services, and remote access is crucial to its emergence. The virtual library includes at least three dimensions: infrastructure, resources and applications, and influential environmental forces (Saunders and Mitchell 1996, 2). Saunders and Mitchell go on to describe the virtual library as a "comforting illusion of a single system" (1996, 13). In the virtual library the distinctions between the OPAC, the scholar's workstation, a database server, and a personal computer become blurred (Saunders and Mitchell 1996, 14). The confluence of the community library space and the personal space of one's own workstation is a vital, controlling characteristic.

For the purposes of this chapter, a virtual library is defined as a portion of cyberspace where most of all of the information and services are presented in a computerized, networked, often hypertextualized environment. How can we distinguish a virtual library from other regions of cyberspace? In a webbed, virtual environment, it may be difficult to distinguish where one library ends and another begins. Use of information in a webbed, virtual environment is not spatially contained. Users grab and use information from various sites on the network. A library without walls is very easy to enter and exit. Nearly all of these definitions focus on collections and content, rather than on services and use. Although a collection could be perceived as just one type of library service, in the early phases of the emergence of virtual libraries it appears that collections, rather than library services, have captured the limelight.

Virtual libraries probably will be more open, transitory, and dynamic than real libraries. Real library use tends to be captivating. In many instances patrons must physically enter the building in order to use the services and information resources. Telephone reference and interlibrary loan services are simply in-library activities undertaken by proxies. In virtual environments, where the exit door is just a mouse click away, how are we going to keep people in the virtual library for any length of time? The concern embedded in this question assumes that a rich, fulfilling exploration of an information space, especially an academic information space, requires some time on task. People will need to dwell in this information space in order to get something useful out of it. User retention within a single search/use session will be a major challenge for the designers and managers of virtual libraries. Atkinson's (1996) examination of boundaries, importation, and circumscription as fundamental to our understanding of information services is pertinent to our exploration of the value and meaning of virtual walls for emerging virtual libraries.

The emerging virtual library has several hypertext qualities. One collection or service can be linked to other pertinent collections and services. Links within bibliographic records and other surrogates for the real thing can be connected easily to other surrogates and to the things themselves. Of course, the paper-based, emerged, real library (PERL) also exhibited several hypertextual aspects. The call number on the card catalog card was a link to a specific, potentially pertinent place on the shelves. The difference between the hypertextual aspects of the PERL and of the EVL is that the EVL hypertext links are more numerous, easier to follow (invoking them requires little physical movement), and more closely tied to the very process itself of searching for information in a net-worked, on-line environment.

The EVL enables a more total immersion (but probably not complete immersion) into the information space called a library. Perhaps the immersion is perceived as more complex and deep because the user is more free to move around in the information space and explore. The notion of total immersion in an information space is not new. Thirty-three years ago, Sutherland (1965) wanted to develop a display mechanism that presented information to all the senses in a form that simulated total immersion in the information environment.

The emergence of virtual libraries raises the question about the importance of spatial characteristics and markers to the process of using information. When the periodicals were housed on the first floor and the books on the second, the spatial characteristics of the building reinforced the distinction between books and periodical articles. The EVL seems to have imploded both the space and the need for spatial characteristics. Ironically, however, to use the EVL increasingly seems to involve metaphorically moving through this weird virtual information environment. Use is movement, and movement is use. If true, how can virtual academic library services survive and flourish in the EVL environment? The power of cyberspace lies in its connectedness. Cyberspace is a continuum, rather than a series of discrete systems that act independently (Woolley 1993, 133).

The display of the interface in many virtual libraries can be tailored by individual users. The type of experience (and hence the outcomes) the user has with a virtual library system may depend on the type of browser software being used, the capacity of the narrowest section of the information network pipeline, the amount of traffic on the network, and other factors beyond the control of library managers. The library no longer has anything approximating complete control over the virtual library environment as experienced by the end user.

As a subset of virtual reality, the notion of a virtual library may contain an inherent flaw. Virtuality is wedded to reality. Virtual reality is an attempt to simulate the experience of reality, grounded in the assumption that real experience is the best possible experience. Although this may be true for surgery (at least for the surgeon), sex, and violence (three distinctly different debates, well beyond the ken of the topic of this chapter), it may not be true for libraries. Virtuality relies on the premise that reality is better, and thus worthy of being emulated. Why should we assume that real libraries are the best of all possible libraries, worthy of unquestioning emulation by the designers and managers of virtual libraries? Why must we assume that use of virtual libraries will be the same old rake's progress toward a clean, well-lighted place?

Virtual library services have been slow to develop. Early development of virtual libraries focused on infrastructure development. When attention turned to content, presentation became the focus of attention. Imagine how many person-hours have been spent mastering the nuances of HTML as a mode of presenting content. The potential of the virtual library as a system for delivering services has only begun to be explored. Part of the sluggishness could be attributed to lack of certainty about what public services will be required in the emerging virtual library. Circulation statistics, turnstile traffic, and interlibrary loan transactions will not mean much (if they retain any meaning at all) in the emerging virtual library environment. The accepted output measures for real libraries appear to have little meaning and significance in the emerging virtual library.

The additional challenges of identifying and measuring outcomes in a virtual environment are added to the enduring problems from the waning print-based library. In the short history of virtual libraries, virtual collection development (such as it is) has preceded and outpaced the development of virtual technical and public services. There may be a parallel with the history of the development of print-based libraries: a library begins with a collection of books (which perforce must be ordered in some way), followed by rudimentary technical services (usually beginning with some form of shelf list, acquisitions list, or catalog, then sprouting into an organized system of creating and organizing bibliographic records that serve as surrogates for the things themselves), then finally by organized public services (again, beginning with circulation, then followed by reference, interlibrary loan, and more specialized public services).

It is difficult to define the ultimate information management system because both the capabilities of the systems and the needs of the users change over time. Perhaps the ultimate goal of any good information system is to support thinking. This means that the system has to provide unmediated access to precisely the needed information at a time and place that the thinker (user) wants it. Saunders (1996) notes that four capabilities are implied in this statement: self-directed access, no spatial barriers, no temporal barriers, and correct information content free of superfluous information. Library OPACs with remote access also overcome spatial and temporal barriers. Compared to a television set they are very difficult to use and, hence, score low on "unmediated access." The search tools are quite powerful but are generally directed to the "cover" and not to the "content" of the information sought and, hence, generally fail in providing "precisely the needed information content." The Internet, the Web, and browsers like Netscape Navigator together form a system that much more closely delivers the desired results. Space is no barrier. Unmediated access is made possible through good point-and-click hypermedia links. Time is no barrier (except during weekday afternoons). However, information content and finding "precisely needed information" (sophisticated search tools) are still the challenges to be overcome. The need for virtual libraries exists.

WHAT ARE OUTCOME MEASURES?

Outcome measures are one way to evaluate libraries and library services. Lancaster (1988, 6–7) identifies four possible reasons for evaluating library services: to establish benchmarks, to compare the performance of several libraries or services, to justify the existence of the service, or to identify possible sources of failure or inefficiency, in order to raise the level of performance at some future date. Evaluating and assessing any library could involve a wide variety of goals, methods, and techniques. Input measures, performance measures, output measures, and outcome measures form a relatively neat subset of all possible methods. All four measurement techniques seem to presume a black box of activity.

Input measures indicate the organizational resources that are put into a system in order to achieve desirable outputs. Input measures will not become obsolete in the emerging virtual library. One obvious, enduring problem with input measures is that, in and of themselves, they are neither an articulation nor a measurement of outputs. Perhaps a less obvious problem with input measures, at least as they have been applied to PERLs, is that they tend to be based on an assumption that the library as an organization does most of the inputting of resources and energy. Attempts to measure the resources input by the end-user population are rare. In the EVL, however, we may witness a fundamental shift in the balance of inputs away from the library and toward the seekers and users of information themselves.

Performance measures tend to concentrate on efficiency. Although they can be either institution-centered or user-centered, library performance measurements, like input measures, usually focus on the institution. Again, user-centered performance measures are rare. Despite Ranganathan's dictum, very few library services and systems, real and virtual, are designed to make information seeking and use as efficient as possible, from the user's perspective. Performance measurement of library services examines how well the service has performed, usually relative to the resources that have been channeled into or committed to the service. Peak service performance is not necessarily seen as the absolute peak performance, regardless of the resources being put into the service, but rather the peak efficiency of the service. Because they have a foot in both the a priori world of inputs and the a posteriori world of outputs, performance measures form a nice bridge over the black box of information seeking and use.

Output measures focus on productivity. They tend to concentrate on small systems or smaller units within a larger system. Output measures pay little attention to overall goals or the effect of output on the surrounding environment of related systems. For example, an interlibrary loan department that concentrates on output measures attempts to achieve the maximum number of transactions possible, given the available resources. The impact of the highest possible volume on end-users, or on other systems within the library, such as collection development, is of marginal interest to an interlibrary loan librarian concentrating on output and output measures. Nevertheless, output measures can point toward the more ineffable outcome measures. For example, output measures are more accurate than input measures when gauging the value an educational institution adds to a student's education. Output measures represent a different way of ascertaining the worth of an institution (Adams 1996).

Outcomes tend to be more difficult to define and measure than inputs and outputs. Outcome measures often are difficult to quantify, but that is not the only source of difficulty. Outcome measures tend to be more closely tied with the mission, goals, and objectives of the service program or the library as a whole. Outcome measures also tend to nest over time, rather than over space. For example, one anticipated outcome for a user of an academic library may be to find five pertinent, retrievable, useful articles on an assigned paper topic. That outcome, however, nests over time within a slightly longer term anticipated outcome of actually completing a good paper, which in turn nests within the outcome of successfully completing the course, which itself nests within the projected outcome of graduating, and so on. Concentrating on outcome measures forces the library management team to consider broader issues of goals, missions, and objectives, as articulated both by the library and the user.

The imminent shift in emphasis (and inputs) from PERLs to EVLs offers the profession a golden opportunity to rethink the entire agonizing project of measuring inputs, performance, outputs, and outcomes. We need to start to think like seekers and users of information. First, we need to realize and emphasize that every seeker/user of information is pursuing her or his present personal project (PPP). The fact that they are presently pursuing it makes it ipso facto their present project. It is a personal project because, even if, like lowly graduate students, they are seeking and using information ultimately to be applied by someone else, they bring a personal style to their behavior, and they have personal reasons for engaging in the present activity. Each PPP involves an intense cluster of activities and behaviors dealing with recorded information.

All PPPs manifest themselves in some sort of work clearing—a kitchen table, a cluttered desktop, or an equally cluttered set of GUI windows. The work clearing is the space, both physical and mental, where the work of the PPP is performed. All users of library systems are engaged in a very subtle process of selectively finding and bringing information into this work clearing. Probably a very small percentage of library users consider the physical library itself to be the primary work clearing. The emergence of virtual libraries offers unprecedented opportunities to facilitate the integration of information into the PPP work clearing. One challenge for designers and managers of virtual libraries is to figure out how to introduce successful library services into virtual environments that are "close" to the virtual work clearings of end users.

If library use is seen as a black box, inputs are the resources (money, time, space, information, human resources, and so on) that get poured into the black box, and outputs are the assembled products, services, and events that emerge from the black box at the other side. Inputs and outputs appear to be directly, if complexly, related—probably causally. If outcomes are those things that are somewhat less quantifiable and more far-reaching than mere outputs, what do we call the things at the front side of the black box that have a corresponding relationship with the inputs? Inputs are to outputs as _____ are to outcomes.

In order to fill in the blank, we need to think of library use as more than a black box. Powell (1994, 261) notes that one key management practice that appears to be absent from many special libraries is the use of effective measurement systems. For knowledge-based endeavors, new measurement systems must provide a process view of the activities within a function, encourage improvement, clarify and communicate the value of the function to senior management, and allow benchmarking comparisons.

Outcomes as a class have various characteristics. Some outcomes can be anticipated, projected, or desired prior to the collection and organization of resources that constitute a library, either real or virtual. Although measuring the outcomes after the fact can be challenging, it is not difficult to identify and articulate the outcomes to be measured. That portion of the job of measuring outcomes already has been done by the designers of the library system. Unanticipated outcomes, however, present a double challenge. First, they need to be identified, then they need to be measured. Usage of a virtual library's collections and services at least points the way toward outcomes. In virtual environments, however, it is becoming increasingly difficult to define and measure usage, despite the increased ability to capture usage statistics.

Any attempt to measure outcomes requires a perspective and must be made from a situated vantage point. A user of an information system may measure and assess outcomes from a different vantage point than would the library manager as a creator and maintainer of the information system. In addition, a creator of a text (commonly referred to as an author) contained in the information system may use entirely different criteria to assess the outcomes of use of her particular text. If a user retrieves an on-line poem from a virtual library which causes the reader to cry bitter tears over the perfidy of humankind, the library manager may assess the outcome as successful (e.g., the reader was able to locate, retrieve, and respond fully to the text), the reader may assess the outcome as successful for different reasons (e.g., a good crying jag serves as a form of catharsis), while the poet may assess the outcome as totally unsatisfactory (e.g., she intended to create a humorous poem). In general, most attempts to assess outcomes have been made from the institutional—library—vantage point. To continue to be useful and meaningful, outcome measures in virtual library environments will need to become more user-centered.

Some librarians are shifting their perspective to represent a user-driven view. The assumption that maximum use of library collections and services is the primary goal is being questioned. Perhaps we need to focus on the process by which library users obtain and assimilate information. The assessment of how well a library succeeds depends on the user as a judge of quality (Nitecki 1996). User-centered outcome measures, furthermore, could concentrate on the manifestation and development of an individual user's navigational skills, the accuracy and development of the user's mental model of the information space being used, or his mental model of the subject domain being explored.

Is measuring outcomes necessarily a quantified, evaluative activity? If browsing or surfing through hypertextual or hypermedia environments will be the dominant way of using virtual libraries, the quantified, evaluative outcome measuring activities we all know and love will probably not be extremely useful or enlightening. Browsing and web surfing are not efficient activities, and perhaps they never will be. Discovering ways to describe and evaluate the effectiveness of browsing and navigational behavior in hypermedia environments will be a challenge for designers and researchers of digital libraries.

Because use of a library rarely, if ever, is an end in itself, it always has been difficult to settle on an agreed list of outcomes—anticipated or serendipitous. The old conundrum about success versus satisfaction continues to apply. The emergence of virtual libraries compounds this problem, primarily because this change will enable library users to engage in post-retrieval processing of information to a greater extent and in a greater variety of ways than was practical in traditional, print-based libraries. Furthermore, use of virtual library services and collections may be radically different than traditional service and use patterns. Measuring the outcomes of virtual browsing and surfing sessions on a computerized, networked information environment is much thornier than measuring the outcomes of more structured (both spatially and intellectually) searching in print-based libraries. The psychological distance between the information resources and the project site will approach zero. Perhaps the ultimate outcome of a virtual library is the same as that of a real library: to facilitate the users' activities that involve learning while working on their present personal information projects. This ultimate outcome can be posed as a question: What work are libraries meant to enable, and what work do they actually enable (Levy and Marshall 1995, 78)?

Library use can be examined in terms of learning outcomes. Seeking and using information is a double learning experience. Users learn about the structure, quality, and content of an information environment while they learn about the subject of their search. User-centered outcome measures could focus on learning outcomes. Librarians who focus on library use as a learning experience have had to include technical expertise and critical thinking skills to the list of learning outcomes (Saunders and Mitchell 1996.)

OTHER WAYS OF THINKING ABOUT LIBRARY PUBLIC SERVICES

The emerging virtual library will require library and information science professionals to explore new ways of thinking about library and information use. We should focus on the enduring mysteries and problems of information use, then fashion public services to serve our understanding of existing technologies, the fundamental nature of information seeking and use, and the anticipated outcomes of the user. A distinction should be made between using virtual library resources to pursue real library services and a completely virtual library environment. An example of the first type would be using Internet-accessible resources to answer a reference question posed by a human being standing in front of a real reference desk. The truly virtual library involves creating an information-seeking and use environment that is not dependent on a humanly perceptible physical space.

The prospects of virtual information spaces necessitates a re-examination of the intent and methods of library public services. The function of any information service is to use available technologies to enhance aggregate value by adding access value to the specific information objects that are inferred to exhibit high content value from the vantage point of particular information users (Atkinson 1996). The fundamental problem with most PERL public services is that, in order to come into existence, they first had to dissociate themselves ever so slightly from core information-seeking activity. For example, Kohl (1996) notes that it has been a failure of the library profession to design (or insist on the design of) effective and highly interactive information systems that necessitated the use of reference librarians. Mediation has been professionally willed into many existing library public services. When a user asks a reference question, attends a library instruction session, submits an interlibrary loan request, or checks out a book, the activities themselves represent a slight hiatus or respite from the rather intense core activity of seeking and using information. In other words, when a library user utilizes public services in a traditional library, mentally and physically she is not at the cutting edge or pit face of her PPP. Public services in PERLs are a bit of a mediated time-out.

One real challenge presented by the emerging virtual library is the daunting task of how to transform public services so that they are less mediated and closer to the cutting edge of the user's PPP. The glory of the virtual library will be not only the remote access that all but removes the barrier of distance between the user and the information, but also that the core components of using a library (the finding aids, the public services, the collections, and the help in general) can be woven back into the core components of present personal information projects—reading, writing, thinking, creating. Examining how several core public services could survive in the EVL reveals some of the central issues.

Circulation is not an essential function of information seeking and use, even in PERL environments. It is easy to imagine a real environment where checking out materials would be unnecessary. If libraries could confidently trust users to return materials when finished, there would be no need for due dates and fines. The public service of circulation concentrates on circulatable items, rather than on the information contained therein. Circulation services exist because real circulatable items possess the ineluctable trait of being difficult and impractical to clone prior to circulation. Although we tacitly encourage users to overcome this trait of paper-based periodical articles by photocopying the original, then leaving the original in the library while carrying away the copy, we sternly frown on this practice with larger documents, such as entire books. This is the real-world corollary to the axiom about information (i.e., that you can give information away, yet still retain it) that the emerging virtual library will allow us to overcome. Circulation services probably will become completely obsolete in the emerging virtual library. The notion of entrusting a copy of a text to a specific user will become moot. Circulation services may be replaced, however, by a system for creating, agreeing to, and managing usage agreements on the fly.

As a potential outcome measure for the EVL, circulation activity is especially unattractive. As noted above, circulation is not an essential aspect of the process of seeking and using information. When circulation services do exist, they are decidedly part of the process, not the outcome, neither for the user nor for the library as an institution. Circulation measures measure circulation. The relationship between the circulation of information-bearing things and the actual use of information remains difficult to comprehend, articulate, and measure. In this sense, measurements of the number and types of files grabbed from a web site do not hold much promise as an outcome measure, because they merely measure a new type of undepletable circulation in a new type of information environment. In and of themselves, web site usage statistics move us not much closer to a complete understanding of how to measure information usage, assuming that information usage is an outcome we wish to measure.

Oddly enough, the public service of maintaining the collection probably will gain importance and thrive in the emerging virtual library. True collection management—encompassing selection, organization, analysis, and maintenance of both the collection and the items within the collection—will become whole and complete in the EVL. Because a collection of electronic documents and hypertext links in a networked environment changes and evolves much more quickly than a paper-based collection of documents, the task of maintaining a collection will become much more central and complex. This sphere of library activity could include periodically checking (probably with little human intervention) URLs and other accepted access standards and mechanisms.

Reference service is in a swoon. One transition problem for reference services is the almost thorough site-specificity of the service as we know it. Even if the user calls in on the phone, we expect her to "go" to the reference desk to ask her reference question. Another transition problem is the fact that reference service is mediated by a trained reference service provider on duty. If in virtual environments, the library and all that it contains is going to move into the work space created by the present personal project, the reference librarian will need to visit each querying user's present personal project clearing, rather than expecting the user to "go" to a virtual reference desk. The work space could become crowded, and the user may need to shoo the reference librarian out of the work clearing when the user feels that her reference need has been met. In general, our collective mental model of how useful reference services could exist in virtual libraries requires much more elaboration and refinement. As Levy and Marshall (1995) note, little attention has been devoted to the additional tools that on-line reference librarians would require to provide service over the Internet.

While unneeded real public services will wither and die, new public services probably will emerge along with the virtual library. One broad area of public service destined to grow by leaps and bounds is post-retrieval processing. In PERLs, once the user has the required information at his disposal, the library as a service organization tends to recede into the background. We assume that the user knows how to read, digest, and apply the information they, with some assistance from the library, have sought, located, and retrieved. With virtual libraries on computerized networks, however, the post-retrieval processing prospects become more complex and challenging. As the distance and distinction between the information space represented by the virtual library and the working space of the PPP diminish, users will demand public services that help them manage and manipulate (despite our impending virtuality, we cannot escape easily from words and concepts based on the Latin word "manus") the information they have found.

The key evaluation criterion in the electronic networked environment is accessibility: can the service make an item accessible to a requester at the time she needs it, from whatever source, in an acceptable form and format (Lancaster 1988, 9)? Users never have been very interested in the ownership of information (Peters 1991, 26). They are much more interested in access and possession. By possession is meant the ability to identify, locate, retrieve, and prepare information for meaningful application at the work clearing of the PPP. The emerging virtual library (or libraries) will not diminish the need for librarians to be cognizant of ownership issues, but we must recognize that it is a professional concern, to which most users usually are uninterested.

In the EVL the information seeker need not remain a lonely hunter. In a virtual, networked environment it may be possible to seek information more as a group process. Group information seeking is difficult to imagine, let alone realize. The ability of a digital library to support communication and collaboration within the user population is as important as its ability to support solitary information-seeking activities (Levy and Marshall 1995, 80). This little shift probably will have profound effects on the nature and reality of scholarly inquiry, teaching, publishing, and communication in general. Reference questions, defined as expressions of moments when one wants to continue moving through an information space, but does not quite know how to proceed, could be posed to a group, rather than to an individual reference librarian. The group of users would fulfill some of their own needs for reference service. The image of the solitary, cloistered scholar is deeply embedded in academic culture, and much of the development work for digital libraries assumes, either implicitly or explicitly, this model of information use (Levy and Marshall 1995, 80). The opportunities revealed by virtual libraries, however, may force us to revise this aspect of our mental model of what use of a digital library will be like.

Anything user- or customer-centered currently has a high, almost hysterical, value, as if we shout out this value at the top of our lungs in the hope of reversing a slippage in service we are unable or unwilling to admit openly. The appeal for user-centered outcome measures being made here, however, may not be just another tired librarian with sore feet climbing onto that bandwagon. Users realize libraries, regardless of the reality or virtuality of the library. Users cause the library to come into being, by seeking, experiencing, and using information. Until the moment of use, all libraries—virtual or real—are pure potentiality. As Levy and Marshall (1995) point out, the most fundamental component of any library is neither the documents (i.e., any enduring communicative record, in any format) nor the technology that enables the creation and maintenance of the communicative documents, but rather the actual work done by library users, as well as the work done by library personnel to support the work of users. Outcome measures should focus on the most fundamental component of the process—the user's bundle of strivings decidedly not vain.

The scope of activities related to information seeking, retrieval, interpretation, and application that result in outcomes is becoming more complex and broad. In the "good old days," in order to retrieve information from a real library, generally you needed to know where the library was located, its hours, its floor plan, how to alphabetize on the fly, how to read, and how to use the basic tools, such as the card catalog and the printed periodical indexes. With the emergence of virtual libraries the requisite skill base has become more challenging. Hardware, software, and connectivity knowledge must be applied to information retrieval tasks. Post-retrieval processing (e.g., downloading and importing) is becoming crucial. Remote access is a 180-degree misnomer for an emerging situation where substantial amounts of needed digitized information are available right at the pit head—the real and virtual place where a person or group of persons pursues a present intellectual project.

Powell (1994) has identified several new ways to measure outcomes. The

Service Level Agreements approach serves as a comprehensive way to collect requirements information, form true partnering relationships with customers, establish robust communication and feedback processes, and create measurement systems that work. The Balanced Scorecard approach advocates the use of a limited number of key measures from four critical perspectives: the financial perspective, the customer perspective, the internal business perspective, and the innovation and learning perspective. It appropriately balances internal and external perspectives regarding performance. The balanced scorecard approach helps a library focus on what it must do well in order to survive and prosper in the face of competition (Powell 1994).

Lancaster (1988, 10–11) emphasizes that, when library services are evaluated, the time of the user must be given sufficient weight. It is erroneous to assume that the user's time is free. The cost of using the library greatly exceeds the cost of the collection, the staff, and the physical or network facilities. Virtual libraries need to gear their collections and services so that the explosion in post-retrieval processing capabilities will be perceived by the user community as a positive advance toward integrating library use into present personal projects, rather than as a further demand on the users' precious time.

Most (perhaps all) library mission statements mention the institutional goal of meeting the information needs of the primary clientele or of the actual user population. Mission statements tend to be user-centered and user-focused. Few institutions (except, perhaps, some departments in the federal government) have the cheek to have institution-centered mission statements. The purpose of an institution is not self-preservation. Outcome measures for the emerging virtual library also should be focused on the user.

CONCLUSION

Technological change often frustrates our mental models, rudely awakening us from our dogmatic slumber. Emerging virtual libraries goad us into healthy debates about fundamental issues. What are the necessary and sufficient conditions for the existence of any library? What are library public services about, and how can they survive and thrive in virtual information environments? What are the anticipated and unexpected outcomes of library use, and how can we measure those outcomes? Paradoxically, the manner in which we engage these fundamental questions perhaps will determine (more so than money and technology) the successful emergence of viable virtual libraries. As Levy and Marshall (1995, 78) point out, expanding our conception of digital libraries should serve to expand the scope and the utility of digital library development projects. "Libraries must move beyond these transitional strategies [e.g., MARC records and on-line catalogs] that automate the old world view and discover new service implementations that add value to the patron in the electronic environment" (Heterick 1996, 169). The depth, earnestness, and playfulness of our collaborative thinking about the future and the ideal will materially affect the robustness of these ethereal, emerging virtual libraries.

The relationship between virtual libraries and outcome measures remains controversial. Crawford and Gorman (1995, 140) suggest that the lack or paucity of national reports of output measures for PERLs is a weakness in the system that provides an advantage for the library managers who are advocating the development of virtual libraries. They argue that if real academic libraries gathered and presented collective statistics that provided a true picture of total library use, the virtual library would be correctly perceived as a hollow sham. Other critics are less strident about the relationship. Powell (1994), for example, is more sanguine. Regardless of who performs the task in the library organization, measuring outcomes is one of many management activities. The emergence of virtual libraries may affect management approaches only in a tactical way, without changing the fundamentals of strategic management. The underlying concepts of customer-focused management will not be profoundly changed by the virtual library. Successful and sustainable measurement systems include a balanced, diverse group of measurement activities that provide a well-rounded view of the process or function being studied. In order to be effective, they also need to include customer data and competitive data (Powell 1994).

As professionals, we need to encourage the creation of information environments where the intellectually distinct tasks of identifying, locating, retrieving, interpreting, evaluating, and applying information become virtually seamless and indistinguishable. The misgivings we feel, however, are caused by the suspicion or fear that seamlessness may breed unconsciousness on the part of users. If the now-distinct tasks of asking a reference question, checking out a book, reading the book, and applying the personal outcome to one's PPP become a relatively seamless flurry of pointing and clicking, what sort of mental model of information seeking, retrieval, and application will emerge, and how can we understand, describe, and teach it? Perhaps we should question the assumption that seamless interaction with information in all instances is an unqualified good. In any world of information, distance may not be entirely bad.

As professionals, we also need to at least question our assumption that a PERL library is indeed the real library, which the EVL attempts to simulate. If we were Platonists, we could argue that the ideal library is the most real library. The mundane library we all grew up with (I assume that the reader is more than five years old) could be seen as a poor imitation of the ideal real library, with the emerging on-line, networked library (what we have been calling the EVL) as a closer approximation to the ideal real library, primarily because it is less constrained by (but not entirely free from) the physicality of mundane libraries and paper-based media. In his analysis of virtual reality in general, Woolley (1993, 119) notes that the physical realm could be understood as a simulation of a deeper, purer reality—a virtual reality somehow more real than mundane, physical reality. To insist that the EVL must simulate mundane libraries—in terms of collections, services, and organization—may be to ignore the liberating aspects of a fully computerized, networked, hypertextual information environment.

REFERENCES

Adams, Mignon. 1996. "Assessment and Academic Libraries." *Library Issues* 16, 5: 1–4.

Atkinson, Ross. 1996. "Library Functions, Scholarly Communication, and the Foundation of the Digital Library: Laying Claim to the Control Zone." *Library Quarterly* 66 (July): 239–265.

Crawford, Walt, and Michael Gorman. 1995. *Future Libraries: Dreams, Madness, & Reality*. Chicago: American Library Association.

Gapen, D. Kay. 1993. "The Virtual Library: Knowledge, Society and the Librarian." In Laverna M. Saunders (ed.), *The Virtual Library: Visions and Realities*. Westport, Conn.: Meckler.

Heterick, Robert C., Jr. 1996. "Are Libraries Necessary in the Revolutionized Environment?" In Gary M. Pitkin (ed.), *The National Electronic Library: A Guide to the Future for Library Managers*. Westport, Conn.: Greenwood Press.

Kohl, David F. 1996. "Public Services in the Revolutionized Environment." In Gary M. Pitkin (ed.), *The National Electronic Library: A Guide to the Future for Library Managers*. Westport, Conn.: Greenwood Press.

Lancaster, F. W. 1988. *If You Want to Evaluate Your Library* . . . Champaign, Ill.: University of Illinois, Graduate School of Library and Information Science.

Levy, David M., and Catherine C. Marshall. 1995. "Going Digital: A Look at Assumptions Underlying Digital Libraries." *Communications of the ACM* 38, 4: 77–84.

Nitecki, Danuta A. 1996. "Changing the Concept and Measure of Service Quality in Academic Libraries." *Journal of Academic Librarianship* 22, 3: 181–190.

Peters, Thomas A. 1991. *The Online Catalog: A Critical Examination of Public Use*. Jefferson, N.C.: McFarland.

Powell, Alan. 1994. "Management Models and Measurement in the Virtual Library." *Special Libraries* 85, 4: 260–263.

Saunders, Laverna. 1996. "A Virtual Interview with Vinod Chachra." *Computers in Libraries* 16, 2: 58–63.

Saunders, Laverna M., and Maurice Mitchell. 1996. "The Evolving Virtual Library: An Overview." In Laverna M. Saunders (ed.), *The Evolving Virtual Library: Visions and Case Studies*. Medford, N.J.: Information Today.

Sutherland, Ivan. 1965. "The Ultimate Display." In W. Kalenich (ed.), *Information Processing*. Proceedings of IFIP Congress 65, Organized by the International Federation for Information Processing, New York, 1965. London: Macmillan.

Woolley, Benjamin. 1993. *Virtual Worlds: A Journey in Hype and Hyperreality*. New York: Penguin Books.

ANNOTATED BIBLIOGRAPHY

Cloyes, Kay. 1994. "The Journey from Vision to Reality of a Virtual Library."*Special Libraries* 85, 4: 253–257. Cloyes describes the creation of a plan for the development of a virtual corporate library at Caterpillar, Inc. A virtual library implies the integration of new electronic services with traditional library services. When developing a virtual library, it is essential to develop a team that has the skills to negotiate a common understanding of the goal. Careful consideration must be given to both cost and value. Develop ways to measure the value of the virtual library in terms appropriate to the larger organization. Support from management is essential to moving from the vision to the reality of a virtual library. No references.

Graham, Peter S. 1995. ''Requirements for the Digital Research Library.'' *College & Research Libraries* 56, 4: 331–339. A digital research library is a collection of electronic information organized for use over a long period of time. It involves merging the missions, capabilities, and histories of research librarianship and computing science. Users will continue to want information that is reliably locatable. Establishing a digital research library requires two kinds of tasks: establishing the digital collection itself, and implementing the tools for using with the collection. In order to meet user expectations, digital research libraries must include authentication and integrity techniques that combine mathematical security with ease of use, public trustworthiness, and privacy protection. Graham focuses on electronic collections and the tools needed to access them, rather than on services. He insists, however, that a library can prove it is an organization, rather than merely a building or a collection, by making an institutional commitment to organize and preserve electronic information.

LaRue, James. 1993. ''The Library of Tomorrow: A Virtual Certainty.'' *Computers in Libraries* 13, 2: 14–16. LaRue argues that a fully automated library (also known as virtual libraries) will not result in the demise of traditional print-based libraries. Virtual libraries are limited to non-fiction information, but consumers also want access to fiction. Library services will become more automated (for instance, cable television and electronic publishing). Virtual means more than just ''fulfilling a similar function.'' Certainly dialing into a computer system and placing a reserve is ''virtually'' the same as going to the library and filling out a card for it. In most respects, especially if the book is not available, a virtual library actually is better, meaning more convenient and efficient.

Lowry, Charles B. 1995. ''Putting the Pieces Together: Essential Technologies for the Virtual Library.'' *Journal of Academic Librarianship* 21 (July): 297–300. Lowry notes that, in the midst of the chaos of the Internet, libraries are among the first destinations local users are likely to visit, because libraries are perceived as stable institutions providing dependable access to authoritative services.

Lyman, Peter. 1996. ''What Is a Digital Library? Technology, Intellectual Property, and the Public Interest.'' *Daedalus* 125, 4: 1–33. Lyman wonders if it is possible to create public institutions like libraries in cyberspace. What kinds of social relations can exist in cyberspace, where information functions as the organizational glue? Any library is more than a collection or a building. It is part of a social strategy to create progress in the sciences and useful arts. Early digital libraries have been designed for the kind of reading where the context for finding information is provided by a question or a problem to be solved, not by the structure of a narrative provided by an author. Lyman notes that the difference between information and a genuine visual culture is that in cyberspace we must rediscover or reinvent the social context of public life, including libraries. Ultimately, digital

6

Users: Their Impact on Planning the Agile Library

Lorraine J. Haricombe

INTRODUCTION

The landscape of higher education has changed significantly in the last few years. Few will dispute the fact that technology has had much to do with this change. At the same time, other changes have occurred that will affect future planning in higher education.

Student demographics have changed in recent years. Shrinkage in the number of traditional college-aged students has led to aggressive recruitment strategies to attract a more diverse group of students. The result is an increasing number of adult students in higher education, many of whom are highly skilled and competent professionals, who return for a second degree or graduate studies. However, they have limited library-use skills and are mostly unfamiliar with the new information technology tools. Their need to become proficient users of the information technologies to do their research means that academic libraries must become sensitive and responsive to these special requirements.

Many universities are investing in distance education programs to sustain themselves. While not a new concept, distance education programs are becoming increasingly popular among adult and part-time students. Corollary to distance education programs is the role of the library to support off-campus students and faculty. To retain their centrality in higher education, libraries need to become active partners with distance education administrators to plan and implement support structures for distance education programs.

Remote access technology has bred a generation of students with high expectations of what technology should do for them. A high school student preparing for college can select, "visit," and even chat with students at a remote school on the World Wide Web. College registration may be done remotely. Term papers may be turned in by "sending" them via e-mail. The convenience of remote access raises the expectations, triggers impatience, and prompts demands for constant access (Kalin 1991, 200). Remote access to on-line catalogs is not a new concept to libraries, however; remote users have grown as a significant segment of the library's clientele. They have expanded and blurred the definition of library users. Understanding and meeting these users' needs underline the service aspect of higher education institutions. Providing appropriate service support to remote users could also serve libraries well economically and politically.

The teaching and learning environment in higher education is changing because technology is impacting the role of traditional pedagogy. Increasingly, academic institutions are restructuring their curricula to move away from the traditional classroom model. They use new technologies to create a collaborative learning environment, known as "learning communities," in which students and faculty work together to create new knowledge. New learning communities exist at several institutions with new ones being planned on a daily basis.

New campus communities are also spawned by interdisciplinary research teams and team-taught courses. Specialized research institutes exist on many campuses to accommodate faculty who engage in interdisciplinary research and teaching. In general, most faculty are not comfortable in library settings beyond their narrow areas of specialization. Moreover, many faculty are unfamiliar with new information technologies. Academic libraries have a responsibility to seek productive partnerships with faculty to emphasize the role of the library meeting their information needs.

Change is all around us. The changing face of higher education shows that more adult students will engage in continuing education at distance education centers. Technology will be their primary means to access information and education. The impact of technology will generate new learning environments with different expectations than the traditional classroom environment. What fundamental changes will these users demand from the library? To remain relevant on their campus, academic libraries need to know their users and be flexible to adjust to their needs.

PARADIGM SHIFTS IN SOCIETY

Baby Boomers

Society is influenced by many factors over several decades. Examples of such factors include war, population growth, and life expectancy. Sociologists agree that the post–World War II years significantly influenced American society.

Described as an era of euphoria, intense patriotism, growth, and prosperity, the postwar years between 1946 and 1964 gave rise to a population explosion. The size of that generation, generally known as the "baby boomers," would impact and radically change the primary stereotypes of society. Jones (1980) describes the impact of boomers as "peristalsis," meaning that they will continue to effect change as they move through life's stages.

The highest number of births in the United States were recorded in 1957 (U.S. Department of Commerce 1975). The gradual decline in birth rates since then would affect society in numerous ways. For example, the bulge of births in 1957 resulted in a record number of college freshmen in 1975. Since then, college administrators have experienced a slow but consistent decline in the number of college-aged students. Collectively, factors such as the baby boomers, longevity, and the declining birth rate have led to a loss of younger students. To compensate for the decline in college-aged students, universities are focusing on another market, namely adult students.

Every generation is a carrier of social change. The baby boomers are characterized as educated, independent, and creative. They are career-oriented with a strong belief in education and the power of information. They embrace intellectual growth and see growth, especially in the area of education, as a cultural value for the late stages of life. The first baby boomers are now reaching middle age and many are back at school for a second degree or graduate studies. Higher education institutions will have to accommodate the transitions needed for these older, nontraditional students. In the same way, academic libraries must account for this phenomenon in their future planning.

The Social Environment's Influences on Education

The evolution of various types of economies, from hunter to agricultural, to an industrial economy, has directly affected societies and their environments. New and emerging technologies have created a personalized economy that is different from any of its predecessors. Information is a key resource in the personalized economy information that can be accessed and used to customize products. New technologies are widely used to market services and products to suit individualistic consumers. Employees in the new economy require sophisticated skills to implement and use the new technologies. Since skills have short-lived relevance in a personalized economy, there is a need for ongoing education to keep abreast of technological advances. The concept of a college education in the personalized economy is changing from a four- to five-year college degree to continuing education from "k to grey." Adults engage in continuing education to acquire the necessary skills to widen their horizons and to enhance their career options. The result is an influx of adult students that is changing the landscape of higher education. Because they work full-time and study part-time they cannot come to class all day. Their demand for access to information and education will challenge colleges and universities to invest in more cost-effective mechanisms than the traditional campus-based mediated teaching model.

Technology

The hype around each technological advancement fuels the expectation that computers can do everything. With each new technology people expect more, and it is reasonable to assume that this trend will continue. Technology, it seems, is both the problem and the solution. The answers to the questions posed by technology can only be answered by more advances in technology.

Technology is widely used in higher education. It does enable more diverse ways of responding to the demand for information and continuing education. According to Massy and Zemsky (1995), colleges and universities cannot become more productive unless they embrace technological tools for teaching and learning. Guskin (1997) claims that the impact of technology will change the learning environment for the student and the teaching role of the faculty. The new technological environment in higher education will engage students in collaborative learning that will make them much more dependent on librarians for guidance. The library will become more central to the students' learning environment rather than auxiliary to faculty teaching.

Student Demographics

The nature of the student population is changing. Today's student body is characterized by heterogeneity in age, race, and socioeconomic background. Only 43 percent are under age 25; one in every six students is nonwhite, more than half (55 percent) of the undergraduates are women, and students from many different socioeconomic groups attend college. Of these, the adult student population is the fastest-growing student population in higher education. The number of adult students has increased by 50 percent in the last 20 years. Between 1980 and 1990 the age group 25 years and older rose by 34 percent. At least 10 percent of all undergraduates are 40 years or older, and among the graduate students, 22 percent are older than 40. Women make up 65 percent of older students (U.S. Department of Education 1995).

Many universities have branched out into the potentially lucrative market of adult students engaged in continuing education. The growth in adult students will require higher education institutions to tailor themselves to accommodate their needs. Typically, adult students have full-time jobs and family responsibilities. Notwithstanding these commitments, older students are usually highly motivated and working in a similar manner as full-time students to succeed academically. Are higher education institutions responsive to the needs of adult students in return for their fees?

To attract students, some colleges and universities are customizing their facilities and curricula. For example, administrators at George Mason University combined the library and student union to meet social and academic needs. They hope that the central location and the varied uses of the facility will build a greater sense of community that will include commuters and adult students. This example reflects a keen sensitivity to students' needs that will hopefully attract students. More important, it is indicative of the changes that academic institutions will need to make to adjust to economic and social pressures. Powerful pressures will force major change. The main issue facing administrators is to take the lead in making responsive changes or be forced into change by external groups (Guskin 1997).

NEW FRONTIERS IN HIGHER EDUCATION

Distance Education

Distance education programs have been established for various reasons including outreach to geographically remote communities (for example, in Australia), meeting the needs of students who cannot afford to study full-time, relieving overcrowded institutions, and to counteract the lack of college-aged students. Its recent popularity is a direct result of the impact of technology.

Between 1992–1993 the number of distance education centers increased by 10 percent. Twigg (1994, 17–20) claims that campus-based, lecture-mediated higher education limits access to education in the very ways that have led to the increased use of distance education. While distance education attracts and provides convenient remote access for part-time students, university administrators face the issue of equity between on-campus and off-campus education. The level of support offered to students and faculty in distance education programs varies among institutions.

The academic library remains a key component in higher education. Without the support of quality library service universities cannot achieve the goal of supplying quality education. The needs of distance learners will require that libraries be actively involved in planning and implementing off-campus programs.

New Learning Environments

The impact of computer technology will have far reaching consequences for higher education. Guskin (1997) claims that the most significant crises colleges and universities will face in the twenty-first century will be the need to restructure higher education. Central to his discussion of change is the role of teaching in the learning environment. Technology allows students to create a learning environment that is less "place centric." They can retrieve information, test simulations, learn independently, or experiment with their peers without interacting with the faculty. Faculty interaction is reduced, resulting in less teaching but more learning.

New and emerging technology has generated other curricular initiatives. These include small, personalized, learning communities in which faculty and students work together to create new knowledge. Learning communities are launched to address issues such as student retention or writing across the curriculum. Others are aimed at specific target groups such as honor students and special needs students. For example, at the University of Washington, the U-WIRED initiative also provides remote connectivity to student athletes. Learning communities provide a collaborative environment in which students and the faculty explore a common theme using an interdisciplinary approach that facilitates communication around shared interests (Matthews 1996). The concept offers a radical contrast to the podium performance of an instructor's expertise. New learning communities provide a curricular initiative to enhance and broaden both students' and teachers' intellectual interaction.

The significance and relevance of new learning communities to libraries cannot be overemphasized. In the new learning environment, the library should assume a leading role on campus that supports information technologies and technologists who are educators to facilitate the student's learning environment.

Interdisciplinary Research

The interdisciplinary approach used in courses spawns new interdisciplinary research teams among faculty. Specialized research institutes focusing on specific scientific or social problems exist on several campuses. "Interdisciplinary groups concerned with topics such as Latin American Studies or Women's Studies constitute [an] example of specialized institutes" (Allen and Sutton 1993, 499). How do libraries respond to these new campus communities? Generally, they have been slow to recognize the impact of interdisciplinary programs on library use and new campus communities. The challenges are many and varied. How do librarians keep abreast of new research methods in the interdisciplinary fields? Who takes responsibility for collection development in "new areas"? Where do the interdisciplinary fields fit into the funding allocation matrix? How flexible are existing classification schemes to fit new interdisciplinary fields? Should reference staff be generalists or specialists? (Searing 1996). Some institutions (for example, the University of Illinois at Urbana–Champaign) have responded to these communities by organizing special collections and hiring librarians with special expertise to address their needs. Other options include sharing a special expertise librarian among member libraries in a region or consortium.

CHALLENGES FOR FUTURE PLANNING IN ACADEMIC LIBRARIES

Planning to meet the needs of users will require some basic information in a number of areas:

- student demographics;
- support services to off-campus students;
- location of remote sites;
- available technology and agility;
- partnership opportunities with other constituents including academic computing departments, corporate, public, and/or other institutional libraries;
- commitment of library support on the part of the University Administration.

Adult Students

Libraries have done a good job of providing services *they* perceived to be important to their users. However, cultural, environmental, and technological changes have impacted the user population and their needs. For example, the growing number of adult students pose different needs that make demands on the traditional roles of librarians. Many adult students return to study after a long absence from college. Comparatively speaking, their computer skills are less sophisticated than younger, full-time students. They require assistance to learn the protocols and search strategies in the variety of information databases available to them. Teaching an adult class differs from teaching traditional college-aged students and it also requires skilled staff who are sensitive to that difference.

Typically, adult students attend evening and weekend classes that place demands on library services during those times (for example, reference assistance, bibliographic instruction, and access to reserve readings). These support services may affect staff work schedules. They may also involve travel to off-campus sites to offer bibliographic instruction. While library brochures at strategic sites are useful handouts for taking home, libraries are increasingly using World Wide Web home pages to provide useful information to guide students and faculty in the use of library resources.

Distance Education Centers

Few institutions have the resources to afford full library facilities and services to students and faculty in off-campus programs. Nonetheless, there exist several models that offer solutions to the problems of delivering library service at a distance.[1] The full extent of technology should be explored to develop library services that respond in diverse ways to the demand for distance education. Off-campus students form a significant segment of the remote users of the library. They have grown as a primary component of the library's clientele that require services such as on-line interlibrary loan requests (or a 1-800 line), document delivery, remote access to full-text journals, electronic reserves, longer service hours, point of need assistance, and longer loan periods.

According to the 1996 ALA report *Electronic Services in Academic Libraries*, many libraries already provide the above named services. Of the institutions that were surveyed, 75 percent offer distance education programs. Their libraries offer a variety of services in conjunction with new technology for distance education faculty and students. For example, the University of California at Irvine uses televideo technology to extend reference services to areas beyond the library. At National-Louis University, bibliographic instruction is offered to off-campus students. Other libraries have formed mutually beneficial partnerships with corporate sectors to address partial needs of distance education students. "Industry supported special libraries have strengths in collections and services which are complemented by those of academic libraries" (Dunn and Grealy 1996, 169). Public libraries too, have become powerful partners to support remote academic sites. Electronic reserves have become popular on many campuses to provide full-text reserve readings to the on-campus and the off-campus students.

Distance education centers offer universities the flexibility to reach out to a lucrative market of nontraditional and adult students away from the central campus. However, library managers must guard the centrality of libraries in the changing landscape of higher education. One of the key challenges to do so is to explore the funding considerations and administrative support that will be required to support this transition.

Remote Users

Academic libraries serve a diverse group of users including students, faculty and staff, local businesses, corporate members, independent researchers, local groups, and residents. Historically, librarians have assumed that they know who their users are. Based on this assumption, they have designed library collections and library services to meet their primary users' needs. Rarely, if at all, were users involved in the design of library services. The result has been libraries that are service-oriented without being very user-centered.

The availability of remote access technology has changed the landscape of users. The definition of patrons is expanding and becoming blurred. Remote users include anyone who uses computer technology to access the library from a distance; they could be anywhere on campus, in the country, or in the world. According to Kalin (1991, 199) many librarians estimate that their remote users are primarily their own patrons. But, she continues, "remote users do not fit into tidy categories. They can be anybody and everybody; their individual characteristics and backgrounds are unknown."

Unlike on-site users, remote users have high expectations. The hype around the benefits of computer technology lead them to believe that anything is possible once they get on the Internet. The exponential growth of more demanding remote users challenges librarians to respond with appropriate support services.

New Learning Environments and Communities

Increasingly, new learning environments are formed through creative use of technology. "Collaboratories" offer new meeting places where faculty and students can meet around a computer terminal to explore information resources on a specific topic. The library seems a natural place for such collaboratories and should assume a leading/central role to help students and faculty locate, evaluate, and incorporate the new sources of information. The importance of partnerships, with computing and other facilities, to design a campus environment that supports the incorporation of information technology into the very fabric of the teaching/learning experience cannot be overemphasized. Partnerships between librarians and course designers will contribute toward a rich and rigorous learning experience inside and outside the classroom. The challenge is to create teams that will enable information technology learning models to become a reality through collaboration and cooperation (Matthews 1996).

This collaborative environment will impact on librarians' roles as facilitators in the new learning environment. It will require continuing education for librarians to become information technologists to support users in the application of the new technologies. Shaughnessy (1996) compares the variety of search protocols to a "kind of Tower of Babel" that must be very confusing to the user. Recruiting or appointing the right persons to assume these roles will affect traditional job responsibilities and relationships.

User Needs and Expectations

The increasingly diverse library user population, combined with new technology require that libraries regularly evaluate their services and products. In an environment of shrinking resources libraries need to evaluate their services to show their effectiveness (or ineffectiveness) in supporting the institutional mission and the users' needs (Millson-Martula and Menon 1995).

Among the popular tools used to gather information about users' needs are questionnaire surveys, telephone interviews, focus groups, and informal channels such as user complaints or suggestions. The complaint form provides an informal mechanism for direct, unsolicited, and personal communication. Library managers ought to evaluate complaints as significant indicators of users' needs. Describing the pros and cons of each survey method is beyond the scope of this chapter. More important is the design of the survey instruments to gather the information they are intended to collect.

Meeting User Expectations

A compilation of information about users will be meaningless unless it is translated into library management decisions to address users' expectations or eliminate obstacles that prevent patrons from satisfying their information needs. Responding to user needs and expectations may require some adjustments in existing services, job descriptions, and organizational structures. In Chapter 2, Rebecca R. Martin discusses the challenges of implementing and managing change.

Many libraries have implemented new services in conjunction with new technologies. While remote access has increased satisfaction among users, they have also elevated the users' expectations. User expectations change continuously, and libraries are usually slow to respond. Libraries are known to have "not focused . . . on the consumer's goals, methods, habits, and motivations" (Osburn 1984, 90). Essentially, libraries have ignored the user. Thomas A. Peters (Chapter 5 of this volume) advocates the need for a more user-centered approach to evaluate library services.

User-Centeredness

While feedback from users (formally or informally) has led to changes in library services or policies, libraries are inclined to adopt a reactive approach rather than a proactive approach to their users' needs. To make responsive changes, libraries will have to follow the example of for-profit organizations; become more user-centered in the design and evaluation of services. Customers have very basic service expectations that include reliability, tangibles, responsiveness, assurance, and empathy (Zeithaml et al. 1990). Darlene E. Weingand (Chapter 7 of this volume) discusses the importance of having a clear knowledge of who the users are and what their needs are. The library's best intentions can go unappreciated if the users' needs are not incorporated into the library's services. Millson-Martula and Menon (1995, 34) remind librarians that "[i]t is crucial . . . not to forget the customers for whom these services exist."

Being more user-oriented may impact how bibliographic orientation or computer training sessions are offered, what information brochures are distributed, what technical support is provided, and who to contact. User needs and expectations may also generate a host of new services and facilities including extended service hours, faxing, electronic reference, electronic reserves, document delivery, study rooms, seating that is conducive to laptops in the library, and other ADA-compliant facilities.

CONCLUSION

Technological advances, student demographics, off-campus instruction, and curricular restructuring have generated significant changes in higher education. These changes will impact the academic library's role and mission in serving its user community. Users realize libraries; without users the library is nothing more than a physical entity with loads of information waiting to be used. The challenge for libraries is to be sensitive to the changing needs of their user population. More important, they also need to be flexible to make responsive changes to address those needs. Failure to do so may render the library irrelevant.

NOTE

1. Special issue on "Off-Campus Library Programs in Higher Education,"*Library Trends* 39, 4 (1991).

REFERENCES

Allen, Bryce, and Brett Sutton. 1993. "Exploring the Intellectual Organization of an Interdisciplinary Research Institute." *College and Research Libraries* 54, 6: 499–515.

American Library Association. 1996. *Electronic Services in Academic Libraries*. Mary Jo Lynch (project director). Chicago: American Library Association.

Dunn, Lisa, and Deborah S. Grealy. 1996. "The Industry Information Center Within an Academic Library: A Case Study." *Special Library* 87, 3 (Summer): 169–179.

Guskin, Alan. 1997. "What Is the Future of Higher Education?" http://www.ala.org/acrl.html.

Jones, Landon Y. 1980. *Great Expectations: America and the Baby Boomer Generation*. New York: Coward, McCann and Geoghegan.

Kalin, Sally W. 1991. "Support Services for Remote Users of Online Public Access Catalogs." *Reference Quarterly* (Winter): 197–213.

Massy, William, and Robert Zemsky. 1995. *Using IT to Enhance Academic Productivity*. Washington, D.C.: Educom.

Matthews, Roberta. 1996. "Technology, Collaboration and Democratic Practice." Keynote speech at ACRL Preconference, New York, July 5. http://www.cni.org/projects.nlc.www/nlc.html.

Millson-Martula, Christopher, and Vanaja Menon. 1995. "Customer Expectations: Concepts and Reality for Academic Library Services." *College and Research Libraries* 56, 1 (January): 33–47.

Osburn, Charles E. 1984. "Issues of Structure and Control in the Scholarly Communication System." *Library Quarterly* 54, 1: 81–93.

Searing, Susan E. 1996. "Meeting the Information Needs of Interdisciplinary Scholars: Issues for Administrators of Large University Libraries." *Library Trends* 45, 2 (Fall): 315–342.

Shaughnessy, Tom. 1996. "Local Databases." A speech given at EBSCO Subscription Services' Executive Seminar for directors of the ARL at the 1996 ALA Midwinter meeting. Reprinted in *Vantage Point*. Birmingham, Ala.: EBSCO Subscription Services, 3–4.

Twigg, Carol. 1994. "The Need for a National Learning Infrastructure."*Educom Review* (September–October): 17–20.

U.S. Department of Commerce, Bureau of the Census. 1975. *Historical Statistics of the U.S.: Colonial Times to 1970*. Washington, D.C.: U.S. Government Printing Office.

U.S. Department of Education. 1995. National Center for Education Statistics. *Digest of Education Statistics*. Washington, D.C: U.S. Government Printing Office.

Zeithaml, Valarie, A. Parasuraman, and Leonard Berry. 1990. *Delivering Quality Service: Balancing Customer Perceptions and Expectations*. New York: Free Press.

ANNOTATED BIBLIOGRAPHY

Drake, Miriam A. 1993. ''Technological Innovation and Organizational Change.'' *Journal of Library Administration* 19, 3/4: 39–53. Describes various factors such as environment, technology, and economics that have affected library services, operations, and organizations. Corollary to this is the effect of technology on customer services. Changes in the services offered are contingent upon the characteristics and expectations of the user population and their use of technology.

Drucker, Peter F. 1995. *Managing in a Time of Great Change*. New York: Truman Talley Books. Describes the challenges managers face to respond to the changes that have already taken place. Provides insights for planning the future of information-based organizations, the economy, and for society in an environment of continuing changes.

Jaros, Joe. 1990. ''Training Endusers/Remote Users.'' *Journal of Library Administration* 12, 2: 75–88. The training of remote users presents both a challenge and an opportunity to reach out to this growing library user group. This article describes the use of a specialized training manual at Texas A&M University Library.

Jones, Landon Y. 1980. *Great Expectations: America and the Baby Boomer Generation*. New York: Coward, McCann and Geoghegan. Generally considered a ''classic,'' the work provides a demographic perspective of the baby-boom generation. The book is useful to understand how the baby boomers have influenced the changes in American society. A related reading on the topic is Cheryl Russell (1993), *The Master Trend: How the Baby Boom Generation Is Remaking America* (New York: Plenum Press).

Kalin, Sally W. 1991. ''Support Services for Remote Users of Online Public Access Catalogs.'' *Reference Quarterly* (Winter): 197–213. This article focuses on users of on-line public access catalogs. It discusses the nature of remote users, the problems they encounter with OPACs, and the ways in which libraries can provide appropriate support services to meet their needs. A related article by Sally Wayman Kalin (1987) appeared earlier entitled, ''The Invisible Users of Online Catalogs: A Public Service Perspective.'' *Library Trends* (Spring): 587–595. The article explored a variety of strategies to enhance support services to the growing community of remote users. Understanding their needs, expectations, and difficulties can help libraries design services to support them.

Millson-Martula, Christopher, and Vanaja Menon. 1995. ''Customer Expectations: Concepts and Reality for Academic Library Services.'' *College and Research Libraries* 56, 1 (January): 33–47. The article deals with the elements that determine expectations as well as the existing gaps that relate to customer expectations and service performance. Provides strategies for management to narrow the gap between the library and its customers.

Parasuraman, A., Leonard Berry, and Valarie Zeithaml. 1991. ''Understanding Customer Expectations of Service.'' *Sloan Management Review* 32 (Spring): 39–48. Based on customer service in the corporate world, the authors argue that the key to success is to understand customer expectations and to respond appropriately. The article describes five dimensions of service and correlates them with customer expectations.

Rosenquist-Buhler, Carla. 1996. "New Partners in Distance Education: Linking Up to Libraries." *Library Administration and Management* 10, 4 (Fall): 220–225. Highlights the importance of partnerships between libraries and distance education administrators to provide support services to distance education students. The article describes profiles of nontraditional on-campus students and distance education students that are helpful to librarians in designing services that will provide point of need access for these students.

7

Marketing the Library Today . . . to Meet the Challenges of Tomorrow

Darlene E. Weingand

Here I am in an academic library with a tight budget, realizing that if the library does not start marketing itself and its services, the campus community may forget all the good things the library offers to the community. What do I need to know . . . and how do I start marketing the library?

The academic library has historically been a complete package: an efficient, convenient, and protective wrapping of information that isolated the information and the librarian and kept the user at arm's length. The quiet stacks provided comfort and solace to the scholar and a sense of order to the librarian. This mystique of hushed learning was cherished by the serious scholar—but a barrier to many casual seekers of information. These old concepts of packaging focused on the library as an institution and continually recreated the image of the library as a building, a physical structure which housed and preserved the records of knowledge.

This image has less and less credibility in today's world, and those who seek to preserve it are doing a disservice to the academic library's effectiveness in the information age. Today, the academic library needs to be viewed as the connecting point between campus needs and relevant information. It is a time of serious change: change that is increasing at an unprecedented rate of speed, fueled by technological developments almost beyond imagination. Information has become a valuable commodity, and the academic library has an exceptional opportunity to position itself on-campus as that point of intersection in transactions that are being viewed as important and relevant.

The process of planning for the changes that are both cause and effect of the information age must incorporate *both* planning and marketing elements, with the intent of connecting excellent products with customer needs and a proactive staff attitude. The outcome has every probability of achieving the desired relationship of mutual benefit between the academic library and the community served.

However, Kotler (1987, 35) contends that "A first requirement for effective, successful marketing in any organization is that the organization have a clear, deeply ingrained appreciation for what marketing is and what it can do for the organization." This chapter will discuss how the academic library can develop that appreciation.

THE FOUNDATION OF LIBRARY MARKETING

Traditionally, the library has been perceived as a public good and has enjoyed a comfortable relationship with its customers. However, such positive regard is difficult to sustain in a time of economic constraints, social change, and technological innovation. When such powerful forces are assaulting the status quo, library managers must have a clear knowledge of who the customers are and what they need—and reporting the library's response to these needs in terms of *perceived customer benefit*. Why is perceived benefit so important? Because all the library's efforts can be disregarded by the library's customers—funders, staff, and users—if they do not *perceive* that the library provides personal benefits that will add value to each individual's life.

How can today's academic library successfully reevaluate its operations in terms of customer benefit? The answer to this fundamental question can be found in the effective use of marketing strategies. Marketing can be viewed as a *process of exchange* and a way to foster the partnership between the academic library and its community. Kotler (1988, 6) states that for this process of exchange to take place, there are five conditions that must be satisfied:

1. There are at least two parties.
2. Each party has something that might be of value to the other party.
3. Each party is capable of communication and delivery.
4. Each party is free to accept or reject the offer.
5. Each party believes it is appropriate or desirable to deal with the other party.

For any partnership to be successful, both partners must believe that the relationship is in equitable balance. Therefore, in order to engage in a successful partnership, both parties need to believe that they are deriving a benefit from the exchange of goods and services. This perception of mutual benefit is essential to sustaining the partnership over the years. If the balance between the two parties is perceived by either partner as unequal or absent, the partnership can be in jeopardy—resulting in effects that range anywhere from declining support to outright termination of the relationship. Therefore, if the academic library is to thrive in this volatile, changing environment, healthy partnerships must be initiated and nurtured with its various constituent groups.

The tools of marketing are central to forging these partnerships. The marketing process is composed of a series of activities that begin with identification of the community's needs and end with communicating back to the community about the library's response to those needs. In between, a full range of planning and marketing efforts carry the entire process forward.

THE CONVERGENCE OF MARKETING AND PLANNING

While marketing and planning can be viewed as independent processes, better results occur if they are combined into a single system. Weingand (1987, 16) states that "There is an appropriateness about the convergence of the marketing and planning processes: either of these two processes, while having intrinsic value, is incomplete without the other in the sense that each amplifies the power of the other and provides a wholeness of purpose and application."

Building a marketing/planning framework that will assist in making decisions works best when developed over a period of time with input from stakeholders— as opposed to reactive coping with existing and emerging crises (Area Library Service Authorities 1989–1990, 12). In addition, as the rate of change continues to produce an increasing number of challenges, it becomes tempting to focus on immediate issues and postpone long-range decisions. But it is this very tendency to focus on today's crisis that presents a dramatic reason for using a marketing/planning framework to inform decisions. In addition to being a powerful managerial tool, marketing/planning strategies can be a strong deterrent to the emergence of a crisis. When planning is done in tandem with marketing, problems are less likely to grow to crisis proportions.

The following sequence illustrates the stages of the integrated marketing/planning process:

- The *marketing audit*, which includes:
    A *community analysis* of the library's *external environment*;
    An assessment of the library's strengths and weaknesses, plus existing practices (*internal environment*).
- Following the marketing audit, the organizational *mission* is determined and/or re-examined.
- Once the mission (and appropriate roles) are in place, the *goals* for the time period are established (for example, one year for the short-range or operational plan; five years for the long-range/strategic plan).

- An *analysis of trends* is made (environmental scanning).
- Measurable *objectives* are developed that will move the library toward its goals.
- *Products* (collection, services, programs) are designed in conjunction with the objectives.
- Analysis of *price* (cost to produce each product) is made to determine product priorities.
- *Action plans* for each objective are designed.
- Distribution channels (*Place*) are designed in conjunction with the planned actions.
- The actions are implemented.
- *Promotion/communication* techniques are developed to communicate the library's responses to identified needs to the community.
- A final or *summary evaluation* and updating is made of all goals, objectives, and priorities. (Note: A *second evaluation* monitors progress toward the goals throughout the operation of the merged systems.)

There is, indeed, an appropriateness about merging the marketing and planning processes. The relationship is somewhat analogous to that of theory and practice: planning sets the conceptual framework; marketing implements the planning directives, creating an environment in which an effective exchange process can take place.

GETTING OFF TO A GOOD START: THE PLANNING TEAM

The marketing/planning process actually begins with the creation of a planning team, a working group composed of representatives from both internal and external constituencies. The team should consist of members of the library staff (including the director) and policy makers/funders plus representatives from customer groups, such as faculty, students, administrators, and staff. Although customer and staff input is frequently sought in typical data gathering, it is less common for such representation to be an integral part of the planning group. Long-range benefits can accrue when those affected by decisions have been part of the making of those decisions. The planning groups that include this range of involvement not only contribute diverse and realistic perspectives, but also develop the "ownership" that is so necessary to the implementation of decisions.

THE PLANNING CYCLE

Once the planning team is formed, the planning cycle needs to be considered; how often will the process come full circle and begin to repeat? Under normal conditions, a planning team can expect to work with small cycles within a larger cycle: operational (one-) year planning within the larger context of a five-year long-range plan. If major change is encountered, either internally or externally, the planning cycle may need to be compressed—particularly in terms of gathering new environmental data.

Operational year planning is an ongoing process, with the next year's planning beginning as soon as planning for the present year is completed. The operational plan is typically tied to the budget development process, and the two processes interact to become the working documents of the library.

The long-range plan, while a five-year projection, is a rolling horizon document. Each year, as a new operational planning effort begins, the long-range plan needs to be reviewed and updated. In this way, the long-range plan forever extends five years into the future.

THE CONCEPT OF EFFORT

If the library staff is not to "burn out," it is critical that those in charge realistically examine the library's size, budget, and resources and, in so doing, determine the appropriate level of effort which will be applied to the planning process. Such an assessment cuts short that temptation to do too much, the outcome of which could create negative staff morale and disinclination toward future planning. The following factors are considered in the determination of level of effort (McClure et al. 1987, 4):

- *Participants.* The more individuals and the more groups represented, the higher the library's level of effort for planning.
- *Resources.* Higher levels of effort call for a proportionally greater commitment of the library staff's time and larger expenditures from the library's budget.
- *Library context.* Libraries serving a community with rapid growth or change, a complex and diverse population, shifting economic conditions, or libraries facing a major change in funding may need to plan at a higher level of effort.
- *Planning purposes.* What the library expects the planning process to accomplish may affect the level of effort chosen for some planning phases.
- *Planning structure.* Libraries planning at a basic level of effort may approach many planning activities informally; but as library complexity increases, the planning structure becomes more formal, thus increasing the level of effort.
- *Planning schedule.* Some libraries may complete their first objectives cycle over a very short time period; higher levels of effort may require 12 to 18 months to complete.

It is important to note that the same level of effort does not have to be present in all phases of the planning process. For example, a major environmental assessment (or marketing audit) may be indicated in year one, but not for the next several years.

THE MARKETING AUDIT

Environments, both internal and external to the library, need to be routinely assessed. Kotler (1982, 185) defines the marketing audit as a "comprehensive, systematic, independent, and periodic examination of the [library's] total environment, objectives, strategies, and activities, [and resources] in order to determine problem areas and opportunities and to recommend a plan of action.'' Almost every word in this definition should be considered carefully by the planning team, with particular attention to the process words: comprehensive, systematic, independent, and periodic.

As introduced above, both the internal and external environments need to be analyzed. The library's existing practices, strategies, activities, and resources (human, fiscal, physical) are part of its *internal environment*, and a profile of strengths, weaknesses, opportunities, and threats (a SWOT analysis) should be made. Also to be considered are organizational climate and structure, communication patterns, and whatever marketing efforts are currently in place.

In terms of the *external environment*, the library has both micro and macro spheres of operation. The micro sphere includes the library's immediate community: faculty, students (both on-campus and from a distance), regulations, administration, and so on. The macro sphere is much broader: the larger environment within which the library operates, but over which little or no control can be exerted (for example, national or regional economic upswings and downturns). The following components should be considered:

- *Demographics.* What are the attributes of the campus community in terms of population, age, gender, educational background, income, range of jobs, and so forth?
- *Geography.* What constitutes the physical landscape, climate, and other physical attributes of the campus and its surroundings? How many students and/or staff members interact with the campus from a distance?
- *Sociology and Psychology.* What individuals and groups comprise the target markets (for example, faculty, students, and such)? What are their preferences and biases? What are the social patterns? How do members of these markets behave under different sets of circumstances or levels of stress? Can probable behavior be anticipated? Where is the power located on campus and how does it flow?
- *Economics.* What is the overall fiscal health of the campus? What is the current climate for growth or retrenchment?
- *Technology.* What hardware is presently on campus? What technologies are customers and/or departments planning to purchase? What use is made of different technologies?
- *Politics.* What is the library's relationship to funding sources, both on campus and beyond? What kinds of lobbying/maneuvering have been done in the past? What worked and what did not?
- *Culture.* What intellectual and artistic activity is present on campus? Are there gaps that the library should attempt to fill? What cooperative ventures could be proposed?
- *Competition.* What campus departments, agencies, vendors, organizations, or individuals provide similar products to those offered by the library? Where do areas of duplication exist? What areas of possible cooperation exist?

Before a marketing audit is initiated, certain fundamental points should be considered:

1. Analysis of the environment is not an occasional activity. While the large data collection is done at periodic intervals, monitoring of the environment must be a continual effort so that trends and changing conditions are detected.

2. As introduced earlier, it is important that environmental analysis be a collaborative effort among library staff, policy makers, and representatives of the library's target markets. This is a learning opportunity for all who are involved and establishes a common sense of ownership. There may be surprises in the data which will alter previously held perceptions on the part of library staff or customers. These surprises may require shifts in expectations, service emphases, and marketing strategies. It is vital that all constituent groups, both internal and external to the library, be involved in the process, and not simply be recipients of a final report.

3. As analysis allows the planning spotlight to fall on those portions of the campus which are less well served, an important next step involves outreach efforts specifically targeted to those individuals or groups. While the marketing audit can admirably profile the campus in general terms, library service succeeds to the degree to which it responds to individual human beings with unique perceptions and needs.

4. Change is with us. At no point during the audit can the data be regarded as static. Even as the environment is being analyzed, the campus is in a state of flux, reacting to political, economic, and social forces. The marketing audit provides a snapshot of today, nothing more. It must be recognized that analyzing the environment is both necessary and never completed. The challenge is to aggressively and positively seek out the avenues for intersection with the campus community.

COLLECTING PRIMARY SOURCE DATA

Once secondary sources have been exhausted, and there are still questions about the campus community to be answered, it is time to turn to primary data collection. No single method works equally well for every library, and the decision must be made as to the most appropriate strategy for assessing the local situation. Sampling is generally used to establish an N (number to be surveyed) of reasonable size, as trying to question the entire population is beyond the scope of any library's resources. Many elementary books of statistics provide both instruction on how to draw a sample and a table of random numbers from which to choose the initial sample digit(s). Once the sample is drawn, the fol lowing methods, used either singly or in combination, can be started:

1. *The Telephone Survey.* The telephone survey can be one of the most effective methods to use. The campus directory and local telephone book (if relevant) can be the source of names to be called. However, if a public telephone book is used, the outcome will reflect a bias, since unlisted numbers are not included. A more thorough approach involves using the computer to randomly generate telephone numbers; many colleges or universities have research labs which offer this service.

2. *The Interview Schedule* (another term for a questionnaire used in a one-to-one interaction) is only as worthwhile as the questions that it asks. Before the questionnaire is put together, the library administration must determine *what it wants to know*. Only

data needed for decision-making should be sought; the temptation to throw in questions because "it would be interesting to know" should be vigorously resisted. Also, since questionnaire design is a learned skill, if the library does not have such expertise on staff, it should seek it elsewhere.

3. *The Mail Survey*. This method differs from the telephone survey in the way the questionnaire is constructed. The questions need to be a bit a more formal, since there is no opportunity for questioning the client's intent—which is possible during the one-on-one interchange of the telephone interview. However, as stressed above, the questionnaire design is crucial and questions must be carefully worded—then pretested.

4. *The Interview*. Another approach entirely is the face-to-face interview of library users (in the library), campus community (in person, outside the library), or both. This method is time-intensive in that a designated and trained staff member or volunteer conducts each in-depth interview. And interview schedule must still be used so that there is an internal consistency to the range of interviews. However, there is also the added benefit for exploration of customer attitudes beyond specified questions.

   This opportunity for individualized information gathering can have unique benefits. Many attitudes and perceptions may emerge that would not have surfaced in a simple questionnaire format.

5. *The Focus Group*. An expansion of the interview is the focus group. Using a trained facilitator, a small group of participants who share some feature or relationship to the library is convened to explore needs and opportunities. No interview schedule of questions is prepared; rather, the facilitator begins with broad, general questions and leads the group to "focus" more and more on specifics as the exercise proceeds. This method can be extremely helpful, particularly for charting future directions.

6. *The Campus Meeting*. The campus meeting offers an opportunity for anyone in the campus community to voice opinions and concerns. However, it is not recommended as a means to reach the indifferent or the nonuser. Participants in such an open meeting or hearing should generally be regarded as "interested parties," since they have made the effort to attend.

A combination of these methods may also be effective. It is the individual library administration's decision as to what seems most appropriate to the local situation. Once the selection of method or methods has been completed, four steps need to be accomplished:

1. *Decide what elements will be covered*. Consider the depth of coverage desired, resources available to conduct the audit, and planning team/staff expectations of anticipated outcomes.

2. *Develop procedures* for collecting both secondary and primary data and monitoring the process.

3. *Collect and analyze the data*. Use secondary sources first and go after primary source data collection where necessary. (Secondary sources are those data already gathered by other campus units, or other agencies. Primary sources involve collecting original data; methods such as surveys and interviews are often used.)

4. *Communicate the results.* Use both written and oral reports and presentations, using graphics and other visually stimulating approaches.

Library professionals who are not politically aware may regard the work of a marketing audit as a frivolous use of staff time. In addition, once the research is done, the results may be filed away without the library achieving the potential for decision-making and political influence that such research represents.

There is little strength in the presentation of library administration–perceived needs and wants to funding authorities, but there is considerable power in the documentation of library requirements by data reflecting campus needs. The marketing audit is a valuable ally in the struggle toward parity of resources.

ANOTHER LOOK AT THE MISSION

Most library staffs have some idea about what the library's mission is or should be. However, not every library has a formal mission statement. Once the environmental data has been gathered through the marketing audit, the library's mission will need to be thought through again. It is not uncommon for the new data to suggest that the mission which is in place, whether formal or informal, is no longer appropriate. The revised mission statement lends form to the process which is to follow: the development of goals, objectives, and action statements.

THE LIBRARY'S ROAD MAP: GOALS, OBJECTIVES, AND ACTIONS

Goals can be defined as where the library hopes to go and what it plans to do: broadly written statements of purpose. They may or may not be actually reachable, but they serve as a focus for the more specific objectives to follow. Well-written goals tend to adapt well to changing conditions. They also reflect library policy, together with the mission statement. It is from the goals that practical and measurable objectives can be inferred.

Objectives are statements of planned behavior that are both measurable and attainable, and which move the library toward a stated goal. They are tools that the library can use to relate to changing environments. The development of parallel sets of objectives creates working documents that can be useful regardless of changing conditions. These alternative sets provide thoughtfully considered decisions regarding foreseen—but hypothetical—situations. One set should address expected conditions; a second set should take into consideration a worsening economic environment, such as a budget cut; and the third set establishes ''blue sky'' objectives, which can take effect in the event of an economic windfall. The very existence of alternative sets of objectives maintains a proactive state of decision-making and, no matter how severe the crisis, the potential waste of reactive, emotional response is eliminated.

The development of *action statements* is the final step in the implementation phase of the planning/marketing process. Each objective, in order to be accomplished, requires a series of completed actions. These actions are both concrete and detailed, usually listed in sequential order. Like objectives, they are measurable, contain a time line, and specify who is responsible for their completion. In other words, action statements provide the working outline of specific tasks which must be executed before the objective is realized.

ENVIRONMENTAL SCANNING

In past years, when an analysis of the library's environment was done, attention was usually focused on the present, with little or no thought of what rapid change might dictate. It is the responsibility of the planning team to monitor trends and probabilities which may influence library operations and to use this information as a screen to filter the collected data. Data concerning what has already been identified can be secured from city and county planning authorities as well as campus planners.

DEVELOPING PRODUCTS TO MEET CAMPUS NEEDS

Once the needs of the academic library's target markets have been identified through the marketing audit, appropriate products can be developed. The library already provides a range of products/services to the campus, including: the collection, reference/information service, hours during which customers may come in and use the collection, access to the catalog via computer, professional expertise, bibliographic instruction, and so forth. Some of these products are traditional and have been in existence for many years; other products have been developed more recently, such as databases on CD-ROM and access to the Internet, to name a few. As customer needs change and as new technologies emerge, the range of products offered by the academic library must shift as well.

The library's products can be arranged within the structure of Product Mix, Product Line, and Product Item. Examples of academic library products can be arranged as follows:

Product Mix

Product Line #1: Collection

Product Items: Books, periodicals, audiovisual materials, dissertations, and so on

Product Line #2: Services

Product Items: Circulation, reserves, interloan, on-line searches, reference service, electronic access to catalogs/databases/full text, World Wide Web home pages

Product Line #3: Programs

Product Items: Bibliographic instruction, displays, lectures

This model puts the various academic library products into context: individual product items sharing common attributes are collected into product lines, and the sum of product lines forms the overall product mix offered by the library to the campus.

EXPANSION AND CONTRACTION

In this time of rapid change, it becomes increasingly important that library managers and staff continually evaluate the products currently being offered in the light of campus needs and developing technologies. The library's products cannot remain the same, with additions during times when money is available, and little analysis of whether the products are still appropriate and effective.

Every product has a life cycle. There is a time for a new product to be added: it will develop and enjoy a period of maturity . . . there will be an inevitable decline due to changing conditions . . . and, finally, there must eventually come a time of decline and possible phasing out. In libraries, this life cycle may be interrupted during the decline phase because of staff reluctance to part with traditional services, and products may ''linger'' long past the point of real effectiveness. Therefore, it is important that products be regularly evaluated during the annual planning cycle, with library staff becoming comfortable with the concept of a normal product life cycle.

Once this evaluation of each present and potential product is completed, those products appearing to be the most appropriate to the library's goals and objectives must also be reassessed in the light of cost and demand. This, however, is not possible until the cost to produce each product is calculated.

WHAT DO PRODUCTS REALLY COST?

It is at this point in the process that cost must be considered. There is no way to ascertain whether a present product should be retained or a possible product developed without knowing the cost that is involved in producing and distributing each product. How can these cost factors be identified? Every business— and the library is no exception—works within both *direct costs* and *indirect costs*. Direct costs are those items that can be assigned directly to specific products, while indirect costs cover items that relate to the library's total operations. Examples of direct costs include rental of equipment and supplies purchased specifically to support that product.

Indirect costs are those budgeted items which are difficult to assign to individual products because they support several (or all) products in the library. Examples include: the daily operation of buildings and equipment, such as utilities, maintenance, and depreciation; supplies that are normally kept in stock; salaries of permanent library staff; and supplemental services, such as campus purchasing, billing, and printing.

No business could offer a product for sale without knowing what costs were involved, yet most libraries have been in operation for many years without this knowledge. While libraries have obviously had budgets, these budgets have typically been arranged in a line item format, and the costs for each individual product have not been known. This has made decision-making difficult regarding what products to offer, which ones to downsize, and which ones to eliminate.

There is another approach to consider when deciding which products to offer, even when information from the marketing audit and relative cost factors are known: *the relationship between cost and demand.* Every present or proposed product should be able to be classified in one of the following categories:

- High cost–high demand (a difficult decision since, although demand is great, the corresponding cost factor is expensive)
- High cost–low demand (an easy decision: phase out)
- Low cost–high demand (another easy decision and a manager's dream!)
- Low cost–low demand (another difficult decision; while the product is inexpensive, customer interest is slight)

Assigning each product to these categories can be very helpful in making product decisions. In terms of proposed products, a trial period can be put in place in order to determine whether appropriate demand will be forthcoming.

It is not easy to decide which products should be offered. However, with adequate cost data, informed and objective decisions can be made within the context of the planning process. Without this data, vital information would be lacking and subsequent decisions would be less well-informed. With the data in hand, a program budget can be constructed.

PROGRAM BUDGETING

The arrangement of costs by product (or program) is known as a Program Budget. Reasons to create a program budget include:

- The ability to compare costs
- The ability to demonstrate how money will be spent
- The ability to identify which products might be considered for elimination if funding were reduced
- The ability to suggest what products might be provided if additional monies were to become available

While it takes more time to develop a program budget than a basic line item budget, that time is well spent. In addition, the sum of each category in a program budget can quickly be inserted into a line item structure, if that is required by the university. When the line item format is required, the library director can use the program budget as supplementary evidence, along with a program narrative.

CHANNELS OF DISTRIBUTION

How can the academic library's customers be connected with the products that they need? In his many writings, Kotler refers to distribution as ''Place''—a term that is appropriately descriptive when the product is available through a single location: a campus library building. The concept of ''Place'' becomes more involved when there are multiple access points, including both physical locations and electronic delivery systems.

Therefore, it is necessary to discuss ''Place'' in terms of product distribution and channels of connection between products and customers. When access is held out as the goal, objectives and actions can be developed to provide distribution channels that meet customer needs in terms of both time and point of use convenience. Certainly, there are costs connected to distribution and access, and judgments must be made as to which channel(s) within a range of alternatives will be selected for each product.

There are nine factors that influence the distribution decision flow from initial product design through the entire life cycle of the product (Weingand 1987). Remembering that access is the goal, these nine factors need to be the framework for discussion:

Factor #1: Quality of Service. Distribution must be considered an integral part of each product, for a product that is not usable is of very little value. This interdependence of product and distribution can be observed in several measures of quality:

- The nature of the information (level of accuracy, language, appropriateness, etc.)
- The format of the product (audio, print, visual, person-to-person, program, etc.)
- The type of access (building, electronic, mail, etc.), and the speed of obtaining the desired information.

Factor #2: Time, Convenience, and Resource Allocation. Client perception of product excellence will be strongly influenced by the personal time expended. The time element can be defined as:

- The time expended by staff in the process of providing information
- The time expended in overcoming physical distance between customer and product
- The real time that service is available to the client

Factor #3: Priorities and Planning. When a framework of marketing/planning guides the setting of priorities, the focus centers on the customer. As introduced earlier in the discussion on the planning team, it is important that customers become ''stakeholders'' in the entire process so that access considerations can be updated as customer needs change.

Factor #4: Human Resource Intermediaries. Access can also be addressed through cooperative ventures between the academic library and other units on or off campus. These collaborations can expand the effectiveness of all participating agencies and decrease areas of duplication.

Factor #5: Number and Location of Outlets. The word "outlet" is used here as a descriptor for any access point: a library building, a small office with a computer workstation, an electronic linkage, and so forth. Such an access point serves as the connection between the customer and the needed information. Customer convenience, as determined by the marketing audit, must be a priority. Both existing and potential service outlets should be evaluated at regular intervals, in conjunction with planning and marketing deliberations.

Factor #6: Technological Delivery and Formats. Technological development is accelerating so rapidly that new distribution possibilities are continually entering the marketplace: cable television, interactive video, computer networks, teleconferencing, broadcasting systems, satellite transmission, facsimile transmission, videotex, and many combinations of these technologies. Information formats are also continually evolving: audio, video, and optical technologies, to name a few. These formats offer expanding possibilities for customers with special learning styles and needs, and are also important in the storage and retrieval of information.

Factor #7: Innovation and Change. All these factors operate within a change environment and the need for innovative responses to change. In order to remain in the information mainstream, the academic library must be proactive in the distribution of information and be receptive to the dynamics of a changing world.

Factor #8: The Finite Life Cycle. The concept of a life cycle applies to products, but also to all aspects of the marketing mix—including cost, distribution, and promotion. All components of the mix have applications that are developed in response to customer needs, have a peak period of effectiveness, decline, and ultimately must give way to more appropriate applications. This natural ebb and flow is likely to accelerate as the rate of change increases.

Factor #9: Positioning. There are two levels of positioning: (1) identifying the market niche for the academic library within the entire range of information providers serving the campus and (2) developing distributed products that also have a unique market share among the many possible competitors for the "business" of the library's customers.

These nine factors are central to distribution decision-making and need to be carefully considered as the library works toward developing customer-centered approaches to information service for the campus.

COMMUNICATING WITH THE CAMPUS: PROMOTION

In library literature, marketing is too often defined in words that really mean "Promotion." However, promotion is one of the last steps in the marketing/planning process: the step that tells the library's customers that their needs have

been identified and how the library is responding. In the marketing/planning process, ''Promotion'' can be defined as ''Communication.''

Communication can be a complex and frustrating endeavor. The standard ''communication model'' includes a sender, receiver, message, and media channel. Also involved is dissonance—those disturbances that can affect senders and receivers and their ability to either transmit or receive a message with clarity and understanding. Dissonance can be caused by a headache, an argument with a family member, a worrisome situation—the list can be extensive. If either sender or receiver is not ''attending'' to their portion of the transaction, inaccuracies and confusion can result.

Therefore, it is also essential that a feedback loop is incorporated into the process in order to determine: if the message was received; whether the same message content was heard by each market group that the library believes was sent; and finally, each audience's response to each message. There are many ways for a communication message to go astray, and feedback is essential to assure that the library's message is both accurate and being received by the desired customers.

If the academic library's communication with customers is to be effective, those customer market(s) that are to be initially targeted need to be identified so that appropriate message content, message style, and media can be selected. Each market group uses specific media channels to get information, and these channels also need to be targeted.

The identification of the library's various customer markets should have already been done in two prior portions of the marketing/planning process: in the selection of the planning team; and as a result of analyzing the marketing audit data. Once the initial customer markets and the appropriate media channels have been selected, targeted messages can be designed that will ''speak'' directly to the appropriate customer groups. For example, it is unlikely that today's college student listens consistently to an ''easy listening'' radio station; messages would be more effectively placed on local stations featuring popular music. Also, the campus newspaper would be a more likely media channel than the community newspaper. The question that needs to be asked is: ''Where does the designated customer group go for information?''

Potential media channels can include: broadcast (radio, television), interactive (campus web page), print (student and local newspapers, popular magazines), and the very effective ''word-of-mouth.'' All of these channels have possibilities for promoting the library's activities. The challenge is to link the specific market group with the most relevant media channel—and then to solicit feedback to ensure that the message has been heard and understood.

EVALUATION: HOW WELL DOES IT ALL WORK?

Evaluation is an essential component of the marketing/planning process. Both *monitoring* and *summary* evaluation should be used to make the marketing/

planning process effective and meaningful. Data collection needs to be correlated to the desired outcome and must be linked directly to the question: "What do we need/want to know to make informed and intelligent decisions?"

This is a time of accountability, with shrinking resources and expanding needs. Documentation with hard data is becoming essential in order to demonstrate accountability. Such documentation also makes comparisons possible between the academic library and other academic libraries of comparable size and activity, and between present and past performance. The importance of documenting the status and quality of library service is very real. Accountability demands it, and the demonstration of the library's impact on campus cannot occur without it.

However, the data may indicate that certain actions need to be taken that may or may not be popular with some staff—such as changes in hours or job assignments—but it is essential that identified changes *do* occur in order to maintain credibility with the campus community.

AND ALL THIS MEANS . . .

It is the focus on customer service, within the context of a marketing/planning process, that will ultimately make the academic library central to the campus community. The marketing/planning strategies presented here can help the academic library become more closely attuned to the needs and wants of its target markets. If the academic library wishes to position itself to move successfully into the next century (and what library does not have this intention!), then using marketing strategies can help enormously in the effort to reach this goal. While existing resources, including staff preferences, are important considerations, they should not be viewed as boxes that prevent the library from achieving its objectives. Creative thinkers learn to think "outside the box."

When the knowledge and skills of staff are framed within an attitude that focuses on the customer, then the use of marketing strategies can have real impact. It is an exciting and challenging time for higher education and for the library functioning within the campus environment. As academic priorities adapt to a changing society, there will come unique windows of opportunity for academic libraries to harness developing technologies and service approaches in support of campus goals.

REFERENCES

Area Library Service Authorities and Indiana State Library. 1989–1990. *The Application of Marketing in Libraries, Phase 2*. Indianapolis: Indiana State Library.

Kotler, Philip. 1988. *Marketing Management: Analysis, Planning, Implementation, and Control*, 6th ed. Englewood Cliffs, N.J.: Prentice-Hall.

Kotler, Philip, and Alan R. Andreasen. 1987. *Strategic Marketing for Nonprofit Organizations*, 3rd ed. Englewood Cliffs, N.J.: Prentice-Hall.

————. 1982. *Marketing for Nonprofit Organizations*, 2nd ed. Englewood Cliffs, N.J.: Prentice-Hall.

McClure, Charles R. et al. 1987. *Planning & Role Setting for Public Libraries: A Manual of Options and Procedures*. Chicago: American Library Association.

Weingand, Darlene E. 1987. *Marketing/Planning Library and Information Services*. Littleton, Colo.: Libraries Unlimited.

ANNOTATED BIBLIOGRAPHY

Kotler, Philip. 1988. *Marketing Management: Analysis, Planning, Implementation, and Control*, 6th ed. Englewood Cliffs, N.J.: Prentice-Hall. The original marketing thrusts are presented within an overall management context. The contents are applied to organizations regardless of profit/nonprofit status.

————. 1982. *Marketing for Nonprofit Organizations*, 2nd ed. Englewood Cliffs, N.J.: Prentice-Hall. This is the original title that transferred marketing concepts from the profit to the nonprofit sectors. It is a seminal work and presents marketing as a set of strategies that can enable nonprofit organizations to operate more effectively.

Kotler, Philip, and Alan R. Andreasen. 1987. *Strategic Marketing for Nonprofit Organizations*, 3rd ed. Englewood Cliffs, N.J.: Prentice-Hall. This second text that targets nonprofit organizations emphasizes the customer, strategic planning and organization, design of the marketing mix, and controlling marketing strategies.

Pratt, Allan D. 1982. *The Information of the Image*. Norwood, N.J.: Ablex Publishing. The nature of the informative process is examined, with a focus on the scope of systems designed to facilitate that process and thoughts about achieving further progress.

Toffler, Alvin. 1985. *The Adaptive Corporation*. New York: Bantam Books. Toffler presents thoughts on how corporations can adapt to a rapidly changing world and become successful in a new environment.

————. 1980. *The Third Wave*. New York: Bantam Books. An "oldie, but goodie" that contains ideas still relevant today. A "must read."

Vaill, Peter B. 1991. *Managing as a Performing Art: New Ideas for a World of Chaotic Change*. San Francisco: Jossey-Bass. Managing is expanded into a function that involves more than cognitive skills and techniques. Library managers can gain fresh insights from this different approach.

Weingand, Darlene E. 1997. *Customer Service Excellence: A Practical Handbook for Librarians*. Chicago: ALA Editions. This look at customer service and customer satisfaction covers a range of aspects, including the philosophy of service, human development, what is excellence, problem-solving, team-building, the language of customer service, strategies for success, and looking toward the future.

————. 1987. *Marketing/Planning Library and Information Services*. Littleton, Colo.: Libraries Unlimited. Marketing and planning are combined into a single, merged process in which the two approaches complement each other and become stronger and more effective.

Weingand, Darlene E., ed. 1995. *Marketing of Library and Information Services* (*Library Trends* issue) 43, 3 (Winter). A complete issue of *Library Trends* devoted to aspects of marketing. Guest authors contribute perspectives on topics such as customers, community analysis, the library's product, costing, distribution, and promotion.

Selected
Bibliography

Connor, Patrick E., and Linda K. Lake. 1994. *Managing Organizational Change*, 2nd ed. Westport, Conn.: Praeger.

Crawford, Walt, and Michael Gorman. 1995. *Future Libraries: Dreams, Madness, & Reality*. Chicago: American Library Association.

Drucker, Peter F. 1995. *Managing in a Time of Great Change*. New York: Truman Talley Books/Dutton.

Faerman, Sue R. 1993. "Organizational Change and Leadership Styles." *Journal of Library Administration* 19: 55–79.

Goldman, Steven L., Roger N. Nagel, and Kenneth Preiss. 1995. *Agile Competitors and Virtual Organizations: Strategies for Enriching the Customer*. New York: Van Nostrand Reinhold.

Guskin, Alan E. 1997. "What Is the Future of Higher Education?" http://www.ala.org/acrl.html.

———. 1996. "Facing the Future: The Change Process in Restructuring Universities." *Change* 28: 27–37.

Harrison, Bennett. 1994. *Lean and Mean: The Changing Landscape of Corporate Power in the Age of Flexibility*. New York: Basic Books.

Kalin, Sally W. 1991. "Support Services for Remote Users." *Reference Quarterly* (Winter): 197–213.

Kelly, Julia, and Kathryn Robbins. 1996. "Changing Roles for Reference Librarians." *Journal of Library Administration* 22, 2/3: 111–121.

LaGuardia, Cheryl, ed. 1998. *Recreating the Academic Library: Breaking Virtual Ground*. New York: Neal-Schuman.

Lee, Susan. 1998. *The New Library Legacy*. New York: Neal-Schuman.

————. "Organizational Change in Research Libraries." *Journal of Library Administration* 18: 129–143.

Millson-Martula, C., and Vanaja Menon. 1995. "Customer Expectations: Concepts and Reality for Academic Library Services." *College and Research Libraries* (January): 33–47.

Nadler, David A. 1990. "Beyond the Charismatic Leader: Leadership and Organizational Change." *California Management Review* 32 (Winter): 77–97.

New Learning Communities. Who Are They? Expectations. CNI's Web site: URL: http://www.cni.org/projects/nlc/www/nlc.html.

Prokesch, Steven E. "Master Chaos at the High-Tech Frontier." *Harvard Business Review* 71, 6 (November–December 1993): 134–144.

Rosenquist-Buhler, Carla. 1996. "New Partners in Distance Education: Linking up to Libraries." *Library Administration and Management* 10, 4 (Fall): 220–225.

Schwartz, Charles A., ed. 1997. *Restructuring the Academic Library in the Wake of Technological Change*. Chicago: Association of College and Research Libraries.

St. Clair, Guy. 1993. "The Future Challenge: Management and Measurement." *Special Libraries* 84, 3: 151–154.

Underwood, Peter G. 1990. *Managing Change in Libraries and Information Services: A Systems Approach*. London: C. Bingley.

Young, Arthur P., and Thomas A. Peters. 1996. "Reinventing Alexandria: Managing Change in the Electronic Library." *Journal of Library Administration* 22, 2/3: 21–41.

Zeithaml, Valarie, A. Parasuraman, and Leonard Berry. 1990. *Delivering Quality Service: Balancing Customer Perceptions and Expectations*. New York: Free Press.

Index

A National Strategy for Managing Scientific and Technical Information, 11–12
Neal, James, G., 17
not-for-profit sector, 11–13, 111
Nordstrom, 5
Noyce, Robert, 7

objectives, 103
on-line bibliographic instruction, 49
OPAC interfaces (on-line public access catalog), Windows GUI, Web, ASCII, 45–46
organizational change, 18–21, 23, 25, 30, 92; deterioration, 24; effectiveness, 19, 24; redesign, 24
organizational improvement, 24; infrastructure, 17; relationships, 17; resistance, 26–28
Original Levi's, 5
O'Toole, James, 20, 26
outcome measures, 66–79; Balanced Scorecard, 74, 78; Service Level Agreements, 74, 78; user-centered, 67, 69–70, 73
output measures, 65, 67
Overcoming Organizational Defenses, 27, 30
Oxford University, 6

packet radio, 49–50; advantages for libraries, 51; drawbacks 51; in developing nations, 58
paradigm shift, 6, 12–13, 82
participative management, 21
partnerships, 89, 93, 96–97
PCS. *See* Personal Communications Services
perceived customer benefit, 96
performance measures, 66–67; user-centered, 66
PERLs (paper-based, emerged real libraries), 61, 64, 66–67, 70–72, 75
Personal Communications Services (PCS), 48, 53
personal digital assistants, 55, 59
personal productivity, 18

personalized economy, 83
Phipps, Shelley, E., 23, 31
planning, 8, 34, 97–99; cycle, 98–99; team, 98
politics, 100
Preiss, Kenneth, 4, 15–16
present personal project, 67–68, 70–71
printing revolution, 6
procedural justice, 28
process of exchange, 96
product development, 104–105
program budget, 106
project teams. *See* teams
promotion, 108
public services, 70–74

redefining libraries, 18
redistribution of resources, 28
reductions. *See* downsizing
remote access, 39, 63, 73, 82, 87
remote users, 82, 88, 92
reorganization. *See* restructuring
resistance to change, 26–28
responsiveness, 5
restructuring, 22–25, 31
retrenchment, 3, 24
Ricochet network, 56
Rosetto, Louis, 7–10
Runkle, Donald, 4, 13

satellite data transmission, 50, 52
scholarly communication, 6, 8, 73
self-responsibility, 22
Senge, Peter M., 28, 31
shared responsibility, 22
Shaughnessy, Thomas, 22, 31, 89
spread-spectrum data transmission, 51, 56
staff, 20–22, 25; development, 18, 21; empowerment, 18, 21–23, 31; input, 54; involvement, 21; roles, 17; stress, 22, 25; support, 54; training, 54
Steele, Patricia A., 18
Sterling C. Evans Libraries, 10
strategic marketing plan, 10
strategic planning, 10, 19, 30
stress, 22, 25, 28

About the Contributors

STEVEN J. BELL is the Director of the Library at the Philadelphia College for Textiles and Science. He writes and speaks frequently about on-line searching, technology topics, and academic librarianship. He is an Adjunct Associate Professor at Drexel University's College of Information Science and Technology, where he teaches courses on on-line searching and business information resources.

CLIFTON DALE FOSTER is Head of the Special Collections Department for the Auburn University Libraries. He was previously Coordinator of On-line and CD-ROM Search Services at the University of South Alabama Library. For five years, Mr. Foster served as a library/archives database management consultant with InfoGraphics Information Services, where he managed numerous grant-funded projects and government/university contracts.

LORRAINE J. HARICOMBE is Assistant Professor at Northern Illinois University Libraries, DeKalb, Illinois. She is a co-author of *Out in the Cold* (1995) and several articles in library journals.

FRED HEATH is Dean of the general libraries at Texas A&M University and holder of the Sterling C. Evans Endowed Chair. He is the former editor of *Library Administration & Management*. He has served previously as director at Texas Christian University and the University of North Alabama.

T. J. LUSHER is the Assistant Director for Automated Library Systems at Northern Illinois University. Her research interest area is the use of technology to meet the needs of library patrons.

REBECCA R. MARTIN is Dean of Libraries at the University of Vermont, where she also is a faculty member in public administration, teaching organizational behavior and human resources management.

W. BEDE MITCHELL is Associate University Librarian, Appalachian State University, Boone, North Carolina. He has authored several articles on faculty status for librarians and management issues in access services.

THOMAS A. PETERS is the Associate Director for Collections and Technical Services at the University Libraries of Northern Illinois University. He is the author of *The Online Catalog: A Critical Examination of Public Use* (1991) and currently is working on another book about computerized monitoring in libraries, the workplace, and the Web.

DARLENE E. WEINGAND is Professor and Director of the University of Wisconsin–Madison School of Library and Information Studies Continuing Education Services. She consults and lectures in the areas of continuing education, marketing, customer service, libraries' futures, telecommunications, and media. She is the author of more than a dozen books and articles.